The Story
of the
Battersea Dogs' Home

The Story of the Battersea Dogs' Home

GLORIA COTTESLOE

*'Sssh! Listen, the lawyer's about
to tell them I've left it all to
the Battersea Dogs' Home.'*

David & Charles
Newton Abbot   London   North Pomfret (Vt)

British Library Cataloguing in Publication Data

Cottesloe, Gloria, *Baroness Cottesloe*
 The story of the Battersea Dogs' Home.
 1. Battersea Dogs' Home—History
 I. Title
 636.7'01'0942166   HV4806.L/

 ISBN 0–7153–7704–3

Photoset and printed in Great Britain
by Redwood Burn Ltd, Trowbridge and Esher
for David & Charles (Publishers) Limited
Brunel House Newton Abbot Devon

Published in the United States of America
by David & Charles Inc
North Pomfret Vermont 05053 USA

ONE BROWN DOG

The Office door closed, dulling the din from the kennels.
'What do you want this dog for?' I was asked austerely,
'House-dog, watch-dog?' I looked at him, gaunt and quivering,
Amber eyes searching mine. 'I want him,' I answered,
'For a friend.' They were satisfied then. They wrote on the paper,
     One brown dog.

Cross-bred he is, not mongrel. Some collie about him:
Surely a collie's tail, all flaunting and plumy?
He still wags it only half-arc. He is doubtful and anxious,
Haunted by eight days' divorce from the graces of living,
In a teeming world where he was a nameless unit—
     One brown dog.

Joyous, fleet creature, graceful and ardent and golden,
Look at him now, as he skims the green like a swallow,
Or lies relaxed with a loving head on my instep.
'For a friend,' did I say? Well, I know what riches of friendship
Were pledged by the three brief words on his Battersea docket—
     One brown dog.

DOROTHY MARGARET STUART

For Bouncer

Contents

1 Man and his Dog

More than five million people have visited the Dogs' Home, Battersea, during its maintenance of an ever-open door to all the stray dogs found wandering in London since its foundation in 1860.

There are three types of visitor. There are those who come full of hope in search of their lost friend. There are those who come to look for a new friend and to offer a loving home to an unwanted dog or to a stray that has remained unclaimed. The third type is the person who comes down out of curiosity, just to have a look at the Home, to see what it is like and what is done there.

Before embarking on the story that lies behind this Dogs' Home, which has become a world-famous institution in the minds of the general public, whether they are dog-lovers or not, a sanctuary for stray dogs that has made the very word 'Battersea' almost synonymous with that of 'dog', we have to ask ourselves some questions. Why is it that these people flock to the Home in their thousands—the figures have remained amazingly constant at about fifty thousand each year—and what is the hold that the dog appears to have over man? What are these strong bonds that seem to have caused their destinies to run together, creating a relationship that has stood the test of time?

In an attempt to answer these questions, it is necessary to go back to primeval times, before recorded history, for the actual origins of the dog are lost in antiquity.

First, a little technical background needs to be filled in. Specialists in zoological classification split the dog family into two lines, the evolution of which appear to have taken a parallel course: the first of these are dogs and wolves, the second are foxes and jackals. All four species are carnivorous animals, and all four have many identical characteristics which make the task of separating and classifying them all the more difficult.

Firstly, the general definition that they share is that they are all pack animals, their young being born in large litters in a helpless, blind and deaf condition after a gestation period of about sixty-three days in holes or lairs. They all have the same number of teeth with identical dentification, and they all have five toes on their front paws and four on their back ones. On each toe is a very strong nail, hard and curved, and totally unlike the sharp, pointed retractile claws of the cat family. There are, of course, many specialised and interesting biological similarities which need not concern us in this short study of man's relationship to dog. A most fascinating thing that is common to all four animals, and which brings them into one large group, is the fact that to a greater or lesser extent they are all capable of inter-breeding. A mating between a dog and a wolf will be successful—indeed in Canada and Alaska a husky bitch is often tethered outside at night in the hope that a wolf will father her whelps and thus strengthen the breed. A mating between a dog and a jackal will also be successful, and even a mating between a dog and a fox is possible, although it is extremely difficult and very rare. What is more, a scientifically supervised mating to obtain an equal mixing of the blood of dog, wolf and jackal has been achieved under laboratory conditions.

Now let us take a look at the distribution of the ancestral stock of the dog all over the world. Going east, we find the jackal, which originated in tropical Asia and has now spread to parts of Africa and to northern Russia. In India there is the rare Arctic fox and also the Indian wild dog, which is a little like a chow chow. In Malaysia and Indonesia there is an animal known as a dhole, slightly bigger than the jackal, with short, bright red fur and tall, erect ears. China, Korea and Japan have a dog that looks and behaves rather like a racoon, having nocturnal habits, and this animal is also to be found in Sweden, Finland and Russia, where its fur is marketed under the name of Japanese fox.

In North America the prairie wolf, also known as the coyote, has spread across the east and north, though the common wolf, *Canis lupus*, has virtually disappeared from the United States, and is only occasionally to be found in Mexico and Canada. The American fox, the eastern grey fox, the black fox and the

American kit fox are also to be found in the States. In South America there is a strange animal known as the maned wolf, which has enormously long legs.

In Africa there are a number of hunting dogs about which very little is known. A breed that has become domestically established in other parts of the world is the basenji, which does not bark but retains the weird high-pitched howl of the wild dog, and whose female comes in season only once a year. In Africa we also find the hyena dog, with high hind quarters and enormous, erect rounded ears. Hyena dogs hunt in packs alongside the hyena, which they closely resemble. Unfortunately, they are becoming the victims of man's almost ungovernable lust for hunting, the result being that their numbers are rapidly decreasing.

Another dog that originated in Africa and appears to go right back to the earliest days of civilisation, and which has become popular in the west, is the saluki, which resembles very closely the long-haired greyhounds that were well known and much valued in ancient Egypt.

In Australia there is the dingo, an animal that comes somewhere between the ancestral dog types and the ownerless street dogs known as pi dogs which are to be found right across Northern Africa and Asia, as far as Japan. Pi dogs differ in type, varying from an animal that looks like a sheepdog, the chow chow type, and a primitive greyhound. Nobody has yet come up with an authoritative opinion as to whether these pi dogs or pariahs are the wild descendants of earlier domesticated breeds, or whether in fact they are exactly the opposite, and are dogs in their earliest stages of domestication.

It must be repeated that the origins of the true dog, our domesticated friend and ally, are buried in antiquity. Our first pictorial sight of it is to be found in the Magdalenian frescoes of Spain, which date from the Mesolithic era, about twelve thousand years ago. The very fact that the dog did not appear in earlier primitive paintings together with bison, boar and reindeer must lead us to suppose that it was the friend of man, and not his prey. Proof would surely have been found in the very early rock and cave drawings of battles had man needed to fight dog and subjugate it through force.

What we do know for certain is that, many thousands of

years ago, nomadic tribes moved along the coasts of the North Sea, gradually settling and forming hunting and fishing communities. The piles of bones and debris that collected around these settlements form extremely important archaeological proof of the way of life of the inhabitants; but what is most important to us in this study of the relationship between man and dog is the fact that many of the bones found lying about have marks upon them that could have been made only by the gnawing teeth of dogs, and by no other creature.

Out of all the researches that have been made, the fact emerges that the dog was certainly the first animal ever to be domesticated, and, what is more, trained; for it is clear that, at a time when horses, goats and sheep were still running wild, dogs were sharing the caves that sheltered man. In England, when the Neolithic camp at Windmill Hill, near Avebury in Wiltshire, was excavated, the bones of a domesticated dog were found. From the position in which they lay, it is evident that the dog had been tame, and was allowed to roam at will in the camp, which was inhabited ten thousand years ago.

It has been pointed out that the dog is a pack animal, but what we may not fully realise until we take thought is that we too are pack animals, and perhaps this is the elusive link that so evidently joins the two species.

It is possible that man originally hunted dog for food, and then, having cornered and captured a bitch either in whelp or already with her pups, decided to rear them as stock. It is easy to imagine him succumbing to the evident charms of those puppies, and from the closer relationship that would then have developed he might have begun to realise the potential of this new relationship. Once taken into man's home to share his hearth, the dog was destined to become his faithful friend, ally and support.

Baron Cuvier (1769–1832), the great French anatomist and naturalist, described the training by man of the dog as 'the completest, the most singular and the most useful conquest ever made by man'. It is beyond dispute that the ownership of property is one of the bases upon which civilisation has been developed, and the dog soon showed that it was capable of guarding the captured prey, the horse and the reindeer, thus making it possible for man to build up a store of possessions for the first time. So the hand-to-mouth nature of man's existence was modified. At last he was able to lay in stores of flesh, food and furs, secure in the knowledge that the guardianship of these treasures would be safely taken care of by his dogs.

Once the dog had been taken into the family of mankind, it then started to assert the characteristics for which it is still so much valued the world over to this day. It barked as a warning, thus warding off enemies. It was the first beast of burden, carrying game, animal skins and branches, later being harnessed to the first primitive form of sledge.

With its keen sense of smell, and being infinitely fleeter of foot than man, it was natural that the next step was for the dog to assist with hunting. This must have proved one of the most difficult lessons of all, for it had to be taught to give up the prey it had caught or retrieved, and this must have gone against its deepest instincts. It also had to be taught to lie obediently for lengths of time on command, guarding the captured animals, an action which, if practised in the wild, would have been tantamount to suicide.

The extraordinary fact that emerges from research is that the taming and subsequent training of dogs appears to have happened more or less simultaneously all over the world.

The development of the dog in relation to its size, shape and coat must have depended almost entirely on which part of the globe it was to be found, the first variations being caused partly by nature and partly by climatic conditions. All dogs must have been natural hunters, but what they hunted would have depended on where they lived. Their geographical position would have determined how much, or, alternatively, how little, protection from the elements were necessary. Where their natural prey were swiftly moving creatures, the dog had of necessity to develop the sort of body that could move even faster and was capable of twisting and turning, its brain developing at the same time so that it was capable of out-manoeuvring its prey. This led to the greyhound-lurcher variations, which use their eyes as they hunt, spotting a fast-moving object from a great distance, and then outpace it, twisting and turning as they do so.

In the cover of the great forests, the dog would have had to depend on its nose for its hunting success, and when its prey lived underground the dog would not only have needed a good nose, but it would also have had to develop digging ability and the kind of conformation that would lend itself to the task. The bigger and fiercer the prey then, *ipso facto*, the bigger and fiercer the dog had to be.

As man's relationship with his new-found friend developed, so he took in hand the task that up to then had been performed by nature, and developed new breeds to suit his particular purpose. The best example of this is the development of the wolf-like shepherd dog which guarded sheep from their natural prey, the wolf. This dog looked so like a wolf that the predator became wary, as it was not anxious to enter into mortal combat with one of its own kind. In the Greek mountain ranges, sheepdogs were developed that looked like sheep, so that when the unsuspecting wolf descended on the fold it found itself routed by a vast woolly monster that it had innocently believed to be one of its stupid ovine prey—a veritable wolf in sheep's clothing.

As man became more and more settled in his habits and intellect crept into his life, so there came about a subtle change in his breeding of dogs, and animals such as the pekinese, the pug and non-sporting varieties of spaniel, intended entirely for decoration and companionship, came into being.

Now we come on to the period of authenticated history, where we are able to study the records of ancient Egypt. The presence of the dog is constantly portrayed, very often as a sacred animal believed to provide protection; later on it appears in hunting scenes, and, later still, it is to be seen fiercely pursuing human foes. Cream-coloured mastiff-like animals wearing savagely spiked collars were set on invading hordes, ancestors of the fierce dogs still abundant in the Taurus mountains, and even now used by the Turks to guard their flocks.

Little by little, in ancient Egypt, it can be seen that the dog became man's friend, graduating to appear in that role instead of being depicted only in hunting scenes. Then came the time when, after death, the dog was embalmed and placed in its own sarcophagus just like its human master. The Egyptians mourned for their dogs, as we ourselves do today, but with a good deal more ceremony, carrying their doubtless genuine grief to extremes by shaving their heads—a practise we are never likely to observe . . .

The killing of a dog became a most serious and punishable offence, which in extreme cases called for the death penalty.

It is interesting to note that evidently the dog in ancient Egypt never occupied a subordinate position. It was a hunting dog, a war dog or a temple guard, while the black slaves and the children were given what was considered the menial task of watching over the flocks.

A look at history all over the world shows us that the important part that dogs have always played in the lives of man is beyond dispute. They appear in the annals of ancient Greece, when Homer tells the touching story of Argus, the dog that loved and was loved by Ulysses. Left behind by the great warrior when he went to war, it was abandoned and lived in the streets, pathetic, verminous and half-starving. Twenty years later when Ulysses returned unrecognised, it was this dog alone, in the extremities of its old age, that knew him before any man. Homer sadly records, however, that the ancient dog dropped dead from the sheer joy of being reunited with his beloved master.

Actaeon, the hunter, was punished for watching Artemis (the Greek counterpart of Diana, Roman goddess of hunting) bathing. He was instantly turned into a stag, caught and devoured by his own hounds.

The citadel of Corinth was suddenly attacked one night and, while the soldiers slept in peaceful oblivion of what was happening, the town was defended by its fifty courageous watchdogs, all save one fighting to the death. That one survivor ran to the gates of the town and gave the alarm, at which the sleeping soldiers awoke, rose to the defence and the attack was then repulsed. This heroic survivor of the brigade of watchdogs was given a pension and a collar of solid silver which bore the inscription: 'To Soter, defender and saviour of Corinth, placed under the protection of his friends.'

We are all familiar with the *cave canem* mosaic from the house of the poet in Pompeii, but there is also a memorial stone still to be seen there in the ruins to a dog that saved its child master from water, fire and thieves. Ironically, it was unable to save the little boy from the volcano, Vesuvius, when its engulfing lava destroyed the town.

In ancient Rome, the dog was the privileged possession of the leisured classes. After the disintegration of the Roman Empire, however, dogs sadly went into the descendent and were to be deprived of the close relationship they had enjoyed for so long

15

with man. They had, perforce, to form themselves into packs, living by scavenging, and thus reverting to a semi-wild state. They went through a long period when they were both scorned and feared, but they survived, and it was their hunting ability that led to their gradual reinstatement; by the fifth century AD they had attained some consequence once more.

It was with the reinstatement of the dog as a friend and joint hunter that medicine began to be practised on the species. Up to then only the Arabs, ever mindful of their intrinsic worth, had bothered to give dogs medical attention. They, in fact, went so far as to perform intricate operations on their most valuable dogs. Medicine, as we know, began as an art, but towards the end of the eighth century AD to cure disease and to ease pain became a ministry, carried out with God's aid. The Church, however, chose to surround healing with mystery, making it into a cult of secrecy and solemn oaths, dogs not being considered of sufficient importance for admittance to its powers.

Most of our knowledge of the part that dogs have played in the lives of men throughout history has, of necessity, come from pictures. A walk through the great art galleries of the world, will provide us with fascinating glimpses of dogs performing in battle or during the chase, at rest under the serving table, and adorning the silken laps of noble ladies. It is especially noticeable how many pictures of royal families from all over the world and throughout the course of history have depicted favourite dogs in their midst, and often in places of great prominence.

In eighteenth-century France, after the Revolution, hunting was no longer the prerogative of the aristocrat, but was a sport permitted to the common man. However, in order to be able to hunt and shoot successfully, he found it essential to enlist the help of a dog. With very few exceptions, the princely packs of hunting hounds that had been carefully bred for centuries had disappeared, and in their place rose up thousands of nondescript animals that would probably remind us of most of those to be found at Battersea, the result of chance matings, with little or no talent either for the chase or for retrieving. It thus became essential to evolve a gun dog that would have either known, or, at any rate, predictable qualities. This marked the start of the breeding of setters, spaniels and retrievers.

There were also the small breeds that either went to ground after their prey or were used solely as pets. A notable exception was the little Welsh corgi, originally bred as a cattle dog. The corgi has been popular with several of our own monarchs: Henry II and Richard the Lionheart were depicted with them many centuries before they became the favourite breed of King George VI and of our present Queen.

Dogs, of course, abound in literature, and the dog-lover cannot help but be moved by Byron's lines: 'When all is finished for the proud son of man, one sees on his tomb what he should have become, and not what he did become, but the value of the dog is forgotten, and the soul he had on earth is refused him in heaven.'

The following lines, also by Byron, appear at the beginning of each Annual Report of the Dogs' Home:

With eye upraised, his master's looks to scan,
The joy, the solace, and the aid of man;
The rich man's guardian and the poor man's friend,
The only creature faithful to the end.

2 The Home's Foundation

The Dogs' Home did not start south of the River Thames as its present name might suggest, but was founded in 1860 in the then middle-class village-suburb of Holloway. Holloway is now a vast amorphous district, cut in two by the Great North Road as it starts its four-hundred-mile journey to Scotland, and its name is perhaps unhappily more associated nowadays in people's minds with the women's prison than with anything else.

The cover of the first report of the newly formed Dogs' Home bore the following words, meant to make a direct appeal to the sympathies of an earnest Victorian public:

The Committee would willingly hope and believe that no one who is capable of appreciating the faithful, affectionate, and devoted nature of the dog, can have seen any of these intelligent creatures lost, emaciated and even dying from starvation, without feeling an earnest wish that there were some means established for rescuing them from so dreadful a death, and restoring them to usefulness.

The person to whom each Annual Report of the Home since then has been dedicated, and whose name lives on at the Dogs' Home at Battersea, is a woman called Mary Tealby, who was undoubtedly the driving force that lay behind the Home's original foundation.

Very little is known of Mrs Tealby, apart from the fact that she was evidently the estranged wife of a timber merchant from Hull. For the last few years of her life, during which time she founded the Dogs' Home, she shared a small house in Islington with her clergyman brother, Edward Bates. All attempts to find out any further details about her life have been abortive, and it is as if a curtain has been drawn over her past. Maybe she would have preferred it that way, happy to be remembered for the one great achievement that has made her name live on.

One afternoon in the early summer of 1860 Mrs Mary Tealby visited a friend, a Mrs Major who lived in a house in Canonbury Square, Islington. This visit was destined to become a historic occasion. On her arrival at the tall Georgian terraced house, Mrs Tealby was not shown into what would have been a heavily furnished Victorian drawing-room on the first floor but was instead taken downstairs into the kitchen regions. Here she was shown a pathetic little form lying in a comatose condition on a blanket in front of the kitchen range, which would have been lit even at the height of summer. It was a dog, almost in the last stages of starvation.

It seems that, earlier in the day, Mrs Major had been walking in the street near her home when she had come across this poor little creature. Filled with pity, and managing to overcome her natural repugnance at the thought of touching so filthy an animal, she had gathered it up and brought it home, where now she was making an attempt to nurse it back to life.

There must undoubtedly have been something about this little waif of the streets that touched the hearts of these two Victorian ladies of late middle-age, inspiring them with a fervour and zeal that was destined to last until the end of both their lives. Together they set about nursing the little dog, and such was their new-found enthusiasm for its plight that within a few days it had been joined by several others they had collected from the streets.

Piecing together the remarkable story of determination and hard work that followed, it becomes evident that Mrs Tealby was the leader and Mrs Major, although originally the prime mover, was more than willing to follow. In the intervals of caring for their new charges, they must have put their heads together and decided that more help must be recruited.

The obvious person for them to approach first was Mrs Tealby's brother, Edward Bates. As a retired clergyman who had been educated at Uppingham and Cambridge and who had held a series of livings in Northamptonshire, he had doubtless made influential friends during the course of his life. Goaded on by his forceful sister, he was evidently persuaded to enlist as many of these friends as possible to help with her new campaign of mercy and succour.

The first prospectus of the Home, published on 2 October 1860, stated that it was appealing for funds to help to run a Home for Lost and Starving Dogs, the following being its Rules and Regulations:

1. Any dog found and brought to the Home, if applied for by the owner, will be given up to his master upon payment of the expenses of its keep.

2. Any dogs lost by Subscribers and brought to the Home, will be given up free of all expense.

3. Any dog brought to the Home, not identified and claimed within fourteen days from the time of its admission, will, by order of the Committee, be sold to pay expenses, or be otherwise disposed of.

4. To prevent dog-stealing, no reward will be given to persons bringing dogs to the Home. The Committee would hope that, to persons of ordinary humanity, the consciousness of having performed a merciful action would be sufficient recompense.

5. It is intended, as soon as a suitable arrangement can be made, to have a place especially prepared for the reception of dogs belonging to Ladies or Gentlemen, who may wish to have care taken of them during their absence from home.

6. None but Governors of the Institution shall be eligible for the Committee, or vote at any meeting of the Institution.

7. A donation of five pounds constitutes a Life Governor, and the yearly subscription of five shillings and upwards an Annual Governor of the Institution, and any Lady or Gentleman collecting small sums to the amount of five pounds will be considered a Life Governor.

Ladies and Gentlemen whose humanity may induce them to send dogs to the Home from a distance, are recommended not to reward the persons taking the dogs until they bring a certificate from the Home that the dogs have been received; such certificate will be given whenever asked for.

This last paragraph was evidently added to deter would-be

thieves, who might all too easily be tempted to snatch a dog in order to get a reward for taking it to the Home.

The first committee meeting of a group of like-minded people was held in November 1860 in the Pall Mall offices of the Royal Society for the Prevention of Cruelty to Animals. This Society had been founded in 1824 and is the oldest animal protection society in the world. Some humanitarians got together by a clergyman called Arthur Broome with the help of one Richard Martin decided that it was imperative that the public should be made aware of the appalling cruelty that was taking place all over this country, and indeed in the world, with animals as the victims. Obviously they could not speak for themselves, and were therefore in urgent need of an official voice to speak for them. One by one the grosser forms of cruelty were made illegal in this country, and new measures were introduced to improve the lot of animals in general, making a start with horses and cattle. These were the obvious choice, as the only law that then existed was Martin's Act which had been passed in 1822, applying only to those animals.

Like most other pioneers and innovaters, the Society had to contend with considerable opposition and mockery. Brutality was the general rule of the day in connection with animals, and the very idea of a Society being formed for their protection was ridiculed. As may be imagined, its progress was slow until 1835, when Princess, afterwards to become Queen, Victoria, always having a lively eye to the suffering of her dumb friends, became its Patron at the early age of fifteen. She thus set an example that has been followed by members of the Royal Family ever since. Gradually the Society gained support as its aims and methods became better known, and soon its activities were to spread out to the provinces from the capital, and then abroad, when it became a model for people with similar concern for the sufferings of animals in other countries.

At the first Committee Meeting of the newly established Dogs' Home, the chair was taken by Lord Raynham. John Raynham, who succeeded his father three years later as the 5th Marquess Townshend, was a well-known devotee of animals and their causes. He was a Deputy Lieutenant and Justice of the Peace in both Norfolk and Middlesex, and he was High Steward and Member of Parliament for Tamworth in Warwickshire. An inscription on the back of a *Spy* cartoon refers to the Marquess as 'the beggar's friend', and stories are told of his concern for animals, and of how he would buy suffering birds and beasts from the unscrupulous street traders that then abounded in London, taking them home to Raynham, the family seat in Norfolk, to be nursed back to health and strength. He seems a most appropriate person to have been Patron and President of the Dogs' Home for more than twenty years.

A dozen people, four men and seven women, formed the first Committee and its honorary officers, under the chairmanship of the then Lord Raynham. Like so many reforming zealots, had they known what they were taking on they might never have embarked on their task. They were:

Patronesses
The Right Hon. Lady Millicent Barber
Lady Wiseman
Lady Duckett
Lady Talfourd
Mrs Phillipson

Committee

Mrs Ratcliff Chambers	Mrs Major
Mrs Hambleton	Miss Morgan
Mrs Jesse	Mrs Tealby
Mrs Liveing	Miss Tennyson*

F H Buckeridge, Esq
William Chambers, Esq
Captain Elliott
Captain Liveing, RN

Treasurer and Hon. Secretary
The Reverend Edward Bates, MA

One cannot help both admiring and at the same time being astonished by the courage and temerity of this group of men and women who could consider undertaking such a commitment in a city that was literally seething with lost and starving dogs that lived in conditions graphically described by *Punch*:

* A sister of the Poet Laureate.

> *. . . foul sludge and foetid stream*
> *That from a chain of mantling pools sends up a choky steam;*
> *Walls black with soot and bright with grease;*
> *Low doorways, entries dim;*
> *And out of every window, pale faces gaunt and grim.*

Sir Arthur Bryant in his *English Saga* paints a vivid picture o
the streets in the 1850s:

> . . . pandemonium was long permitted in the sacred name
> of liberty. The drivers of the twopenny buses, growing in
> numbers as well as in girth, raced each other through the
> City, while their stripe-trousered 'cards' or conductors ran
> shouting beside them, sometimes almost dragging unwill-
> ing passengers into their vehicles. The pavements were
> blocked with long, rotating files of wretched men encased
> in huge quadrilateral sandwich boards, and the narrow
> streets with advertising carts towering ever higher like
> moving pagodas in the attempt to overshadow one
> another. Vans stuck fast between the stone posts that still
> served to mark the footways; vendors of vegetables with
> wheelbarrows and ragged organ-grinders paraded the
> cobbled gutters . . . beggars, their clothes caked with a
> layer of phosphorescent grime, to exhibit their sores and
> destitution. Within a stone's throw of the heart of London,
> Leicester Square, formerly the home of great artists, was a
> 'dreary abomination of desolation'. In its centre a headless
> statue, perpetually bombarded by ragged urchins with
> brickbats, stood in a wilderness of weeds frequented by
> starved and half-savage cats.

But there were not only 'starved and half-savage cats'—there
were also dogs darting in and out of streets that were bursting
with all the people going about their varying business, amid a
pandemonium of noise, strident calls from street pedlars, wails
from the beggars accompanied by the rattle of the tins which
they shook for alms; the clip-clop of hooves and the rattle of
heavy-wheeled vehicles, combined with the bewildered bellows
and forlorn baas that came from the cattle and sheep on their
way to Smithfield for slaughter.

Through this chaotic scene scurried a multitude of dis-
ease-ridden dogs, seeking pathetic scraps of sustenance from
the piles of rubbish and ordure that lay everywhere, on every
street corner. Savagely attacking one another over a crust of
bread, the dogs were capable of fighting to the death for a scrap
of meat that still clung to a stinking bone. Covered with sores,
verminous and hideous, this army of starving animals haunted
the streets, homeless and certainly unloved. So familiar were
they in the tumultuous London scene that few people had really
spared a thought for their plight.

By the time of that first Committee meeting those two redoubt-
able ladies, Mrs Tealby and Mrs Major, had already extended
their kitchen kennels, and had started a dogs' home of sorts
that had been running successfully for six weeks.

After searching in the neighbourhood of her Islington home,
Mrs Tealby had eventually come across a mews with stables
running between the Caledonian and Holloway Roads, and
this she had quickly and roughly converted into kennels for her
growing band of rescued dogs, the stableyard itself serving as a
run. A resident keeper was engaged, and a house in the adjoin-
ing road was rented for him. He was not only expected to take
charge of the animals, he also had to answer questions from the
people who brought them in and from all the people who came
hopefully to see if they could find their own lost dog; in addition
he had to keep the necessary records.

Sometimes it seems as if certain people have been placed on
earth by the Almighty to fulfil a purpose. Such a man was
James Pavitt, the first servant of the Dogs' Home, who joined it
from the start in 1860, and was destined to remain with it until
his death in 1883.

On being brought into the premises, the animal was allotted
a name which was chosen by Pavitt from a list of good old tra-
ditional English dogs' names—such as Spot, Fido, Rusty,
Sandy or Towser. This name was entered in a book under a
number, the corresponding tin number being then hung round
the dog's neck on a collar. Thus duly registered, the dog was
given a place in a trough, basket, box, cage or tub, such place
being chosen according to his temper and also dependent on his
general condition of health. This too was done by Pavitt.

This original procedure has served as the pattern for the

reception of a dog right up to the present day. The practise of naming the dogs had, however, to cease very early on owing to the pressure of numbers.

At the outset, dogs were kept for at least fourteen days before being sold or 'otherwise disposed of', this being a euphemism for the drop of prussic acid that was placed on the tongue of the unsuspecting animal by the skilful and dexterous keeper. The ladies concerned with the day-to-day running of the Home could hardly bear the thought of a single one of their beloved canine refugees being destroyed, but they were obliged to agree that there were obvious cases when immediate destruction was the only humane way of dealing with an animal that had been maimed, or was seriously injured or diseased.

It was not long before the rule that started life as 'Any dog brought to the Home and not identified and claimed within fourteen days from the time of admission will, by order of the Committee, be sold to pay expenses, or otherwise disposed of' was modified to: 'That the number of dogs that have been in the Home longer than fourteen days be kept down as nearly as possible to forty.' Even so, this new edict meant that the numbers of dogs in the mews at any one time was likely to be between sixty and seventy, and such quantities presented almost insuperable problems. First there was the problem of housing them, and next was the provision of their food; but by far the biggest headache of all was the nightmare of providing the money to finance such a project.

A year after the foundation of the Home, the owner of the Holloway mews, a builder called Mr Marriott, told Edward Bates on what terms he would continue to make the premises available to the Committee. As it would obviously be necessary for him to build up the walls all round—he had already erected three pens to serve as an infirmary for which he had charged eight pounds—and he would also have to erect substantial gates, he stipulated that the charge would be £120 for the first year, and £100 per annum thereafter.

Happily, however, all sorts of offers of help, both financial and practical, flooded in, and the first prospectus issued by the Committee contained no fewer than 171 names from all spheres of society, ranging from those of His Imperial Highness The Prince Louis Bonaparte, The Dowager Countess of Essex,

Admiral The Hon. Sir Fleetwood Pellew, Lady Olivia Sparrow, Sir Lionel Smith, Bart., Lady Elizabeth Villiers and General and Mrs Vansittart, down to a touching little list of well-wishers—Poor Puff, Nettle and Charlie, 'Pompey' (an old pet), Jacob Faithful, Whisky and Fido, Some Little Children, Three Friends, and Whittington. A Mr Carlton MacCarthy made a cast of a begging dog to be used as a donation box. Six were ordered costing one pound each, and a picture of the model was used in several of the annual reports.

Mrs Hambleton, who was a founder member of the Committee, offered to pay the rent of a receiving house in the West End of London, and enquiries were instituted to find something suitable. However, when a place near Oxford Circus turned up it was found that the rent would be in the region of eighty pounds a year, and this was far and away above what Mrs Hambleton had in mind—it must be remembered that a general servant's wages in those days were in the region of ten pounds per annum—and it was certainly beyond the means of the Committee, who were having a hard enough time to make ends meet without adding to their already substantial commitments. The idea was not to be implemented for several years.

A leading veterinarian, Mr Kidd, delivered a lecture for the benefit of the Home but, sad to relate, it resulted in a loss of very nearly five pounds. Mr Kidd happily vindicated this unsuccessful bid to help the Home by publishing a glowing article about it in *The Veterinarian*.

By and large, however, the establishment of the Dogs' Home had been greeted by the press with jeering mockery, in much the same way as had been lampooned the establishment of the RSPCA. Sentiment, the press considered, was out of keeping with the atmosphere and general feeling that then prevailed. The leader of the anti-Dogs' Home campaign was *The Times*, but when approached by the Secretary of the Home, that august newspaper bluntly refused to publish a letter written by him in its defence. However, a version was later printed by *The Standard* and *The Morning Post*, papers that were evidently more tolerant, or perhaps more prepared to enter into controversial correspondence. However, journalistic help was nigh, and of the highest calibre, for none other than Charles Dickens took up the cudgels on behalf of the struggling little Home.

Charles Dickens was a journalist pure and simple; a finder of facts and a reporter of life as it was currently lived. He set out to give his public a vivid picture of contemporary life, and he certainly succeeded in his aims. 1859 had seen the first issue of a journal called *All The Year Round*, published and edited by Dickens, which succeeded an earlier venture of his, a twopenny weekly called *Household Harmony*. *All The Year Round* started with the serialisation of Dickens' own novel, *A Tale of Two Cities*, followed by *Great Expectations* and then, some years later, *Our Mutual Friend*. The journal happily was an immediate success and, within three months, not only was it financially solvent but it had earned enough to pay its founder five per cent interest on the money he had put into it, leaving him with £500 in the bank as clear profit.

In its issue of 2 August 1862 there was an article called *Two Dog-Shows*, which compared graphically and movingly a visit to the prize Dog Show, forerunner of the now world-famous Crufts Dog Show, at the Islington Hall, followed by an immediate visit to a dog show of a very different sort only a mile away, the not long established little Dogs' Home in Hollinworth Street. Dickens' reforming zeal rings out through the words of this whole article, which at the same time is full of humour and pathos.

It has been said that every individual member of the human race bears in his outward form a resemblance to some animal; and I really believe that (you, the reader, and I, the writer of these words, excepted) this is very generally the case. Everybody surely can with ease point among his friends some who resemble owls, hawks, giraffes, kangaroos, terriers, goats, monkeys. Do we not all know people who are like sheep, pigs, cats, or parrots; the last being, especially in military neighbourhoods, a very common type indeed? Let anyone pay a visit to the Zoological Gardens with this theory of resemblances in his mind, and see how continually he will be reminded of his friends . . .

But what is more remarkable is, that there is one single tribe of animals, and that the most mixed up with man of all, whose different members recall to us constantly different types of humanity. It is impossible to see a large collection of dogs together without being continually reminded of the countenances of people you have met or known; of their countenances, and of their ways.

In that great canine competition which drew crowds some week or two ago, to Islington, there were furnished many wonderful opportunities for moralising on humanity. It was difficult to keep the fancy within bounds. With regard to the prize dogs for instance (to plunge into the subject at once), was there not something of the quiet triumph of human success about their aspect? Was there not something of human malice and disappointment about the look of the unsuccessful competitors? Was there not a tendency in these last to turn their backs upon the winners, and to assume an indifference which they did not feel? There was a certain prize retriever, and a more beautiful animal never wagged tail . . .

Great monster boar-hound, alone worth a moderate journey to get a sight of; gigantic neighbour of the pomeranian with your deep chest, your pointed nose, and your sable fur; sweet-faced muff from St. Bernard, whose small intellect is what might be expected of a race living on the top of a mountain with only monks for company; small shadowy-faced Maltese terrier; supple fox-hound; beloved pug; detested greyhound of Italy; otter-hounds that look like north country gamekeepers—each and all I bid you farewell and proceed yet a little further on my way through the suburbs of North London.

Curiously enough, within a mile of that great dog-show at Islington there existed, and exists still, another dog-show of a very different kind, and forming as complete a contrast to the first as can well be imagined. As you enter the enclosure of this other dog-show, which you approach by certain small thoroughfares of the Holloway district, you find yourself in a queer region, which looks, at first, like a combination of playground and mews. The playground is enclosed on three sides by walls, and on the fourth by a screen of iron cage-work. As soon as you come within sight of this cage some twenty or thirty dogs of every conceivable and inconceivable breed, rush towards the bars, and flattening their poor snouts against the wires, ask in their own peculiar and most forcible language whether you are their master come at last to claim them?

For this second dog-show is nothing more nor less than the show of the Lost Dogs of the Metropolis—the poor vagrant homeless curs that one sees looking out for a dinner in the gutter, or curled up in a doorway taking refuge from their troubles in sleep. To rescue these miserable animals from slow starvation, to provide an asylum where, if it is of the slightest use, they can be restored with food, and kept till a situation can be found for them; or where the utterly useless and diseased cur can be in an instant put out of his misery with a dose of prussic acid;— to effect these objects, and also to provide a means of restoring lost dogs to their owners, a society has actually been formed and has worked for some year and a half with very tolerable success . . .

At the Islington dog-show all was prosperity. Here, all is adversity. There, the exhibited animals were highly valued, and had all their lives been well fed, well housed, carefully watched. Here, for the most part, the poor things had been half-starved and houseless, while as to careful watching, there was plenty of that in one sense, the vigilant householder having watched most carefully his entrance gate to keep such intruders out. At Islington there were dogs estimated by their owners at hundreds of pounds. Here there are animals that are, only from a humane point of view, worth the drop of prussic acid which puts them out of their misery . . .

29

Was it purely an over-indulged fancy that made me discern a great moral difference between the dogs at the Islington Show and those at the Refuge in Holloway?

I must confess that it did appear to me that there was in those most prosperous dogs at the 'show', a slight occasional tendency to 'give themselves airs'. They seemed to regard themselves as public characters who really could not be bored by introductions to private individuals. When these last addressed them, by name too, and in that most conciliatory falsetto which should find its way to a well conditioned dog's inmost heart, it was too often the case that such advances were received with total indifference, and even in some cases I regret to say, with a snap. As to any feeling for, or interest in, each other, the prosperous dogs were utterly devoid of both.

Among the unappreciated and lost dogs of Holloway, on the other hand, there seemed a sort of fellowship of misery, while their urbane and sociable qualities were perfectly irresistible. They were not conspicuous in the matter of breed, it must be owned. A tolerable Newfoundland dog, a deer-hound of some pretensions, a setter, and one or two decent terriers were among the company; but for the most part the architecture of these canine vagrants was decidedly of the composite order. That particular member of the dog tribe with whom the reader is so well acquainted and who represent the great and important family of the mongrels was there in all his—absence of—glory. Poor beast, with his long tail left, not to please Sir Edwin Landseer, but because nobody thought it worth while to cut it, with his notched pendant ears, with his heavy paws, his ignoble countenance, and servile smile of conciliation, snuffing hither and thither, running to and fro, undecided, uncared for, not wanted, timid, supplicatory—there he was, the embodiment of everything that is pitiful, the same poor pattering wretch who follows you along the deserted streets at night, and whose eyes haunt you as you lie in bed after you have locked him out of your house.

To befriend this poor unhappy animal a certain band of humanely disposed persons has established this Holloway asylum, and a system has been got to work which has actually, since October, 1860, rescued at least a thousand lost or homeless dogs from starvation . . . It is the kind of institution which a very sensitive person who has suffered acutely from witnessing the misery of a starving animal would wish for, without imagining for a moment that it could ever seriously exist.

It *does* seriously exist, though. An institution in this practical country founded on a sentiment. The dogs are, for the most part, of little or no worth. I don't think the Duke of Beaufort would have much to say to the beagle I saw sniffing about in the enclosure, and I imagine that the stout man who owned the smaller terriers at the show, would have had little to say to the black-and-tan specimens which mustered strong in numbers, but weak in claims to admiration, in the shut-up house . . . The 'Home' is a very small establishment, with nothing imposing about it—nothing that suggests expense or luxury. I think it is rather hard to laugh this humane effort to scorn. If people really think it wrong to spend a very, very little money on that poor cur whose face I frankly own often haunts my memory, after I have hardened myself successfully against him—if people really do consider it an injustice to the poor, to give to this particular institution' let them leave it to its fate; but I think it is somewhat hard that they should turn the whole scheme into ridicule, or assail it with open ferocity as a dangerous competitor, with other enterprises for public favour . . . At all events, and whether the sentiment be wholesome or morbid, it is worthy of record that such a place exists; an extraordinary monument of the remarkable affection with which English people regard the race of dogs; an evidence of that hidden fund of feeling which survives in some hearts even the rough ordeal of London life in the nineteenth century.

Here, then, were voiced the sentiments of that great writer who was to be lauded and honoured by people in all spheres of life; he was to dine with the Prince of Wales, and later he had a long private interview with Queen Victoria herself. She gave him a presentation copy of her own book, *Leaves from a Journal of our Life in the Highlands*, bearing the modest inscription in her hand: 'From one of the humblest of authors to one of the greatest.' She begged him, on his refusal of any other title, to accept

the nominal distinction of a privy councillor. Small wonder that
the fickle tide of public opinion started to turn, and the Home
was carried on to a new and more respected level.

In 1863 Mr Marriott, the builder-owner of the premises, asked
the Committee whether they would like to consider buying the
whole property outright for the sum of £1,030. Although their
financial position was not yet really sufficiently sound to war-
rant their decision, the Committee jumped at the offer. Marriott was offered a down payment of £550, and was asked to
allow the remaining £480 to be left as a mortgage, instalments
to be paid off at the rate of £20 each year. Eventually, a contract
was signed when, after some pressure from Marriott, the down-
payment was increased to £600. The Committee resolved that,
now it was a property-owning concern, then should the society
be dissolved its property should be sold and the money thus
produced be given as an outright donation to the Royal Society
for the Prevention of Cruelty to Animals, which body had done
a great deal to assist the actual setting up of the Dogs' Home,
not only by practical help, but also by the fact that by its activities public conscience had already been roused to the fate of
animals.

The local paper, *The Islington Gazette*, must have had an editor
who combined humane ideas with vision, for it supported the
struggling little dogs' home from the start. In 1863 it carried a
description of a bazaar held in aid of the home which was
attended by 'the Countess of Essex and several other persons
of distinction'. 'Not only did they attend,' went on the report,
'but they also seemed well aware of the humane object for
which the Bazaar was held.'
It is a delicious example of Victorian local-newspaper
reporting which deserves to be quoted:

> The ladies who presided at the stalls were inde-
> fatigable in their exertions for the 'poor doggies' who,
> were they aware of such kindness, might be expected to
> 'bow' and 'wow' eternal gratitude to their friends.
> A grand pianoforte was hired from Messrs Hopkinson,
> Regent Street, upon which for several hours on both
> days Mr H. R. Bird (who gained so much éclat by his

A 'Dog Show' of a different type: the dogs at the first home at Hollinworth Street

The first keepers were not built for strenuous exercise

An innovation: a fleet of motor vans that were to become a familiar sight in London

performances during the Exhibition [this would have been the Prince Consort's Great Exhibition of 1851]) played most popular pieces to the manifest delight of his auditors. It is due to Mr Bird to say that his services were entirely gratuitous. Several others, both ladies and gentlemen (amateurs), sang and played most agreeably.

The Islington Gazette finished its notice about the Bazaar; echoing Dickens's sentiments:

This description cannot be concluded without the hope being expressed that still greater assistance will be given to this novel but useful charity that is now patronised by many titled, wealthy and eminent individuals. It is trusted that before people condemn or sneer at it, that they will make themselves acquainted with the whole design—a simple matter—if they wish to know the truth—and then they could not fail to see much wisdom as well as policy in it, and thus be taught the folly and injustice of decrying what is good from feelings of prejudice alone, the disposition to do which, be the subject what it may, is one of the commonest marks of a narrow or thoughtless mind.

In 1884, the following year, two new innovations were made at the Home. One was the establishment of the practice of naming a kennel after the donor of a sufficiently large sum of money. This was started by a Miss Pennington who asked if she could have a kennel named after her if she gave the money to maintain it. This practice has been continued to the present day, when a donation of a hundred pounds or more carries with it the right to have a plate fixed above the door of a kennel, bearing the donor's name, or, if preferred, that of a favourite pet. The second, and more practical, innovation was the engaging for a small fee of the services of a veterinary surgeon. The first one to be employed by the Home was a Mr Gowings, who, in the first place, was asked to superintend what were described as 'the sanitary arrangements' of the Home.

At the same time, the Committee decided that the time was ripe for a position to be created of Superintendent to the Home. Pavitt the keeper's hands were more than full with the practical and sheer physical day-to-day running of the place, and he simply did not have time, nor probably the ability, to deal with what were becoming quite sophisticated matters of administration. Mr James Johnson was therefore taken on and was known as the Manager.

1865 was a fateful year, for it saw the lingering illness and ultimately painful death from cancer of Mrs Mary Tealby, the woman who was responsible in the main for the very existence of the Home. Sad though her death was, it did at least come at a time when she was able to see the fruits of her early struggles, and so she must have died happy in the knowledge that the Home was in good hands and on a much more secure footing that it had been hitherto.

A few months after Mrs Tealby's untimely death the first approaches were made by the Committee to the Police, and this was to prove one of the most important things they ever did. Letters were sent to Sir Richard Mayne, Commissioner of the Metropolitan Police, and also to Lieutenant-Colonel Fraser, Commissioner of the City of London Police, asking that a notice should be posted in all police stations giving instructions that stray dogs should be sent to the Home, or to one of the three receiving houses that they had by that time been able to set up in different parts of London. (The receiving houses were at Bowling Street in Westminster, Arthur Street, off the King's Road in Chelsea, and in Southampton Street, Bethnal Green. At these agencies, dogs were taken in from anyone who had found them, and they were kept there until it was possible to transfer them to the main Holloway home.)

The records do not tell us whether it was in fact these approaches that were responsible for the Act of Parliament passed in 1867 empowering the police, and the police alone, to deal with the problem of stray dogs, but it would seem likely. In effect, this Act made every police station in London a receiving house, thus relieving the Dog's Home of what was proving a very expensive responsibility for maintaining theirs, and it meant that all their resources could now be devoted to the main Home.

The police, however, were being let in for much more than had originally been envisaged and, within the year, overwhelmed by the extra work falling on their shoulders as direct result of the Act, they were to make a devastating public statement to the effect that any dog picked up by the police as a stray would be destroyed forthwith.

The Committee of the Dogs' Home was horrified and took immediate action. The Rev G. T. Driffield, a cousin of the Marquess Townshend, and Mr James Johnson, the fairly recently appointed Manager, were sent off post-haste for a further interview with Sir Richard Mayne. They took with them an impassioned appeal pleading that dogs seized by the police should not be dealt with in such a summary, and indeed savage, way, but that all of them should instead be sent to the Dogs' Home by the police at the end of a statutory three days' grace that had originally been allotted to stray dogs by the Act.

Fortunately Sir Richard was both a sensible and an intelligent man, for he quickly saw the advantage to the police of this proposal. He expressed himself only too pleased to enter into an agreement whereby the Dogs' Home would undertake all the new statutory duties of the police, and from then on there were daily deliveries of dogs to the Home by the police. Two years later, in 1870, a firm and binding contract was entered into.

That contract was to form the blueprint of all future ones, and they have continued in more or less the same form with certain financial differences. In the first place, the police undertook no financial obligation, apart from a nominal donation of £10 a year, whereas now they take full responsibility for the cost of keeping the dogs for the first week. This leaves the Home with more funds, which enables them to prolong a dog's stay if necessary until a good home is forthcoming.

So, by statute, dogs are kept at the Home for seven days and, if at the end of that time they remain unclaimed, they become the absolute and legal property of the Dogs' Home, which is empowered to do with them whatever it thinks fit. This obviates any legal problems that can and sometimes do arise should the original owner turn up after a dog has already left the home, or has had for some reason to be destroyed.

At the time that the Dogs' Act was brought in, the press were continuing to support the Home, and the following article appeared in a publication called *Aunt Judy's Christmas Volume for Young People*, edited by Mrs Alfred Gatty—author of *Parables from Nature*, etc.—an annual that contained also such fascinating-sounding articles as 'Confessions of a Naughty Little Boy', 'Foundling Willie' by Agnes Strickland, author of

Lives of the Queens of England, together with poetry and articles on natural history.

> *The rich man's guardian and the poor man's friend,*
> *The only creature faithful to the end.*

They will work for us, and die for us, and, after we are dead, lie on our graves for months, or even years. They *have* done so. So are we not bound to treat them well and kindly, better than all other creatures, for the love and service they give us so gladly?

So have begun to think lately some kind people in London where dogs' misery, like human misery, reaches its worst limits. But the dogs have not been drinking nasty spirits, or spending their bread-money on tobacco, or doing everything they ought not to, like most of those poor masters of theirs. The dogs' troubles are never their own fault. And yet there they are by hundreds, in those endless streets of huge London, starving and without shelter, till their misery ends by their dying in some lonely corner into which they have crept. You can hardly go down a great street in London without seeing one or more of these miserable creatures. Sometimes it is a curled-up mass of dirty fur on the mat by a shop door, so still that it might be dead, but for a convulsive shiver now and then. It is generally a mere mass of skin and bone, and lies there trying to sleep away its hunger and misery. Speak to it, and it looks up with so wistful and imploring a look, that you cannot bear to leave it without doing anything for it. And yet, what can be done? You cannot adopt every cur-casual tramper-dog you come across. A short time ago, it would have been very hard to know what to do; but, thanks to those kind people I have alluded to, there really is now something to be done. The homeless and starving dogs have got a place to go to, if they only knew it, where they will be taken in and 'done for', as lodging-house people say, if only some one would please to put them in the way of getting there.

All you have got to do, to do a very kind act, is to put the poor dog, when you have found him, in the charge of some human casual, whom you will be sure to find within ten yards of the spot, giving him the address of the nearest depot, where he is to take the dog, and from which will bring back a printed form, filled up with the date of the dog's coming. A shilling left in the hands of any one in a shop on the spot, to be claimed on showing the receipt for the dog, will insure its getting there, and, perhaps, be a kindness to the bearer . . .

Nothing else could be done, for the poor creatures accumulated faster than the funds; and, after all, not many come to this fate, for most of the dogs, even if they have lost their owners past finding again, get set up in life with new ones. The Institution is, in fact, becoming quite a dogs' register office. The keeper, who is very well fitted for his place, and very kind to his charge, knows so well the different qualifications of his protégés, that he nearly always picks out the right dog for the right person, according to the list of requirements given him . . .

We asked if those experts, the dog-stealers, did not avail themselves of the chance of getting valuable dogs by coming to claim fictitious lost dogs; but the keeper seemed to think no dog-stealer could possibly escape his penetration, and he takes care to give no dog up to any one until he sees by its manner it knows him; he can tell in a moment from a dog's way of greeting a person. Sometimes a dog going to his or her new master bears this little printed petition tied to his collar:

The Petition of the Poor Dog to his new Master or Mistress upon his Removal from the Home.

Pray have a little patience with me. There are so many of us shut up together here that the keeper has no opportunity to teach us habits of cleanliness. I am quite willing to learn, and am quite capable of being taught. All that is necessary is, that you should take a little pain with me, and kindly bear with me until I have acquired such habits as you wish. I will then be your best and most faithful friend.

Advice

When a dog goes to a new home, care should be taken to prevent his escape until he becomes used to it.

A dog must not be expected to act as a guardian until he has learnt to distinguish, all the members of the family from strangers and to

feel that his master's home is his own; he will then, no doubt, when
occasion requires, be ready to defend both his master and his home.

. . . If people are not very particular about pedigree, which really does not much matter in a house-dog, and want to have a good choice of them, they could not do better than go to the Home and adopt a casual. They can call him a terrier or a bull-dog, or whatever their consciences will allow them. One of the latter dogs, a real *bull-dogue*, was brought in not long ago by two boys, who had seen him run over in the street, and who had borrowed a barrow, in which they had carefully placed him, and wheeled him, by turns, all the way to the Home.

He was dreadfully injured, but, with all the pluck of a bull-dog, he never moaned or whimpered in his pain; the injuries were internal; he lay very quiet, and died that night. Poor injured animals are constantly being brought in by people who have found them in the streets. All get their bones and bruises attended to, and in time get set on their legs again, unless their state is very bad indeed—then prussic acid ends their sufferings. Mange also condemns them to take that dose, for it would run through the place in a very short time.

Two poor little casuals had just been brought in. They lay curled up, all skin and bone, sleeping off their troubles, as they generally do for two days and nights at a stretch, when they come in in that state. Very often they are too weak to get up on the plank bed, and have to be lifted on. Sometimes their feet are bleeding and cut, from having run, perhaps for days, searching for their lost masters . . .

For the dogs, thanks to a large legacy, have been buying their own premises lately; but they had not quite money enough for it. Please help the poor dogs! Think what Dash or Tiny's feelings would be if they had lost you, and were homeless and starving; pity the hundreds who are now astray, and send a small subscription now and then to that famous institution, the 'Temporary Home for Lost and Starving Dogs'.

During the first few years, the Home accepted also a number of dog boarders, a point they had stressed in their first prospectus, as it was felt that such a practice would serve a double purpose. While bringing in a certain amount of revenue—pitifully little judging by the list of charges—it was hoped that it would foster interest in the work of the Home. It was not long, however, before the Committee realised that the disadvantages were very much outweighing the advantages. An increasing number of dogs were being left for months on end, their owners disappearing into the blue, the bills remaining unpaid, and finally the dogs themselves having to be treated as strays. Eventually a demand was made for a month's board in advance, and it was not long before the practice of taking boarders was abandoned altogether.

3 The Move to Battersea

By the end of that first decade, the Dogs' Home at Holloway was getting well known and reasonably well established financially. It had also, more or less, overcome the early prejudices it had received both at the hands of the press and from sections of the general public. However, now a new and what was to prove a major problem was presenting itself that was giving the Committee reason for justifiable amount of concern.

A volley of complaints, with attendant writs, were raining about their heads concerning the disturbance caused by the general comings and goings to the Mews in Hollinworth Street and, more particularly, about the volume of noise.

There can be no doubt at all that the local residents, who, up to the founding of that Dogs' Home, had been living in what was a quiet little backwater, had right on their side. They faced a continual bombardment of noise caused by the incessant barking and howling of the dogs, to say nothing of the pandemonium caused by what had rapidly mounted to a yearly intake of up to ten thousand dogs, many of which needed to be reluctantly dragged, or even forcibly carried, into the mews. Once they were in the pens with their metal tag hanging forlornly around their necks, the miserable creatures lost no time in lifting their noses to the heavens and venting their sorrows in long drawn out howls, in which they were immediately joined by their many companions in distress, the result being a hideous and ear-splitting canine chorus.

Small wonder, then, that the initial patience of the locals, tinged possibly with interest and some curiosity, had changed rapidly to wrath, as what had hitherto been their peaceful neighbourhood was rent asunder by such chaotic conditions of confusion and deafening noise. The din did not come in occasional bursts, which would perhaps have made it slightly

42

more bearable, or at regular intervals as it does from a Hunt Kennels, for instance, where the noise is more or less predictable: the noise from the Dogs' Home was almost incessant, rising to a grand crescendo at feeding-times, and even continuing far into the night.

At first the Committee, dedicated band of enthusiasts that they were, tried to ignore the complaints, pretending to themselves that nothing was amiss. After all, they themselves paid only periodic visits to the Home and did not live in the immediate neighbourhood, so they did not have personal experience of the prevailing conditions brought about by the advent of such an institution. But it was not long before they were obliged to turn round and face facts. What they were forced to realise was that it might be necessary to close the Home down altogether unless something drastic were done—and done immediately, without waiting for such things as Special General Meetings, which could lead only to further delays.

So a subcommittee was formed immediately under the chairmanship of the Hon William Byng, second son of the 1st Earl of Strafford. He had married Flora Fox of Wellingborough in Northamptonshire, which is probably where he had met the Rev. Edward Bates, and so become drawn into the affairs of the Dogs' Home. He had also a local connection in that his sister had married the Member of Parliament for Tufnell Park, the constituency in which Hollinworth Street lay. The other members of this sub-committee were Mr Parkinson, Mr Nugent and Mr Warriner.

Theirs was neither an enviable nor a simple task, for it must have been difficult to know where to start to look for a suitable site in the rapidly growing metropolis that would measure up to the exacting requirements laid down by necessity in their brief. First and foremost, it would have to be of a suitable size, allowing not only for the Home as it already stood but also for a certain amount of expansion. It had to be both moderately central and easily accessible, preferably by both road and rail. It was, of course, imperative in view of the reasons for the move that it should be situated in such a place where it would not be likely to cause any nuisance, nor give rise to any complaints of the sort the Committee was seeking to escape. And, above all, it had to be within their reach financially.

It is sad that there remain no records of the channels they

used to find the site on which the present Dogs' Home stands; but it is clear that the small subcommittee must have gone into action with the utmost speed and efficiency for, in no time at all, they were able to report back to the main Committee that they had found what they considered was just the place.

This was a triangular piece of ground for sale for £1,500 not far from Battersea Park; this, they thought, would be ideal for their purposes. The site was bounded on two sides by the London and South-Eastern Railway, with a station nearby, and on the third by the main Battersea Park Road, down which the 'buses ran. The inhabitants of the nearest houses were likely to find more cause for complaint in the noise coming from the railway and main road than from a Dogs' Home standing in the middle, which should be virtually unnoticed.

The Committee immediately went down to Battersea en masse to make a general visit of inspection, and as a result of their visit a deposit of £100 was put down at the beginning of May 1870.

The money for the purchase of the actual site was borrowed from the London and Westminster Bank of St James's Square, the Bank, which, under the present name of the National Westminster Bank, still handles the financial affairs of the Dogs' Home. This loan was secured by the land at Hollinworth Street, where they had recently managed to clear their debt to Mr Marriott.

It is not made clear in the records of the Home just how the Committee intended paying for the necessary buildings, but a tender was accepted from Messrs Thomas Tully of 13 Regents Row, Daltson, for £1,680, and the work was put in hand straight away. Doubtless, urgency being the essence of the matter, the Committee were prepared to take a risk, and were willing to undertake personal guarantees for the sake of their heart-felt cause.

The borough of Battersea extends to 2,307 acres, ranking fourteenth in size among the Metropolitan boroughs. It is well endowed with open spaces which include not only Battersea Park but also large portions of Clapham and Wandsworth commons. It has a river frontage of some three miles, and is divided into nine wards.

Just before the original foundation of the Dogs' Home in

Holloway, the land on which Battersea Park now stands was a dreary waste, which had, within related memory, been known as Battersea Fields, notorious for its costermongers, gipsies, roughs and the worst characters in and around London. On Sundays it really came to life, with prize-fights and dog-fights; it was even, owing to its lonely and comparatively remote situation, selected as a meeting-place for duellists. The memorable encounter that took place between the Great Duke of Wellington and the Earl of Winchilsea on 21 March 1829, happily without injury on either side, took place on Battersea Fields. The Earl, having escaped the Duke's shot, himself fired into the air, and then tendered his apology, his refusal of which had led to the duel in the first place.

The population of Battersea, which was around the 12,000 mark during the eighteenth century, remained fairly static for many years; but the coming of the railway in 1838 brought with it a great band of labourers who settled themselves around the terminus and the railway depot at Nine Elms. Factories were soon to spring up along the river bank, as more and more of it was reclaimed, and so an urgent need for homes for workers was swiftly created. In 1877 the Victoria Dwellings Association was to open blocks of flats intended as models of dwellings for artisans and labourers to replace the slums that had been condemned in other parts of London under a Housing Act passed in 1875; sadly, the famous market gardens were soon to be swallowed up by the new developments, although even as late as the 1950s there were still some delapidated farm buildings standing near the Dogs' Home.

4 Problems

The opening of the Dogs' Home in its new premises at Battersea took place quietly and without fuss. The dogs in care at the time were moved across in vans hired for the occasion, and Keeper Pavitt and his family went into a small house that had been taken for them nearby.

The local inhabitants of the borough were almost unaware of the advent of this new venture concerning stray and unwanted dogs in their midst, so engaged were they with their own problems and difficulties.

In 1871, as we have seen, Battersea was a rapidly growing parish, although the main population explosion did not take place for another ten years or so when the massive slum clearance was begun and the dwellings made necessary by the growing industries were built. This was before the time of borough councils, which did not come into existence until the end of the century; boroughs were therefore still under the rule of what was known as a Vestry, which drew its members from every ratepayer in the parish. The Vestry was by no means an elected body, nor indeed entirely a representative one. The Vicar took the chair at the meetings which were held in the Vestry room of the Parish Church at Battersea, in common with those held throughout the country. Feelings tended to run very high at the meetings, and debates were of a stormy nature, language being used that was sadly out of keeping with the ecclesiastical surroundings. Votes were taken by a show of hands, and, should a poll then be demanded, the churchwardens were obliged to go all round the parish knocking on every door to find out how each ratepayer wished to place his vote.

These conditions were bound to lead to a certain amount of turmoil, so it is not surprising that the Dogs' Home appeared on the scene virtually unheralded and unsung.

The Committee of the Dogs' Home, who had shown that they were capable of swift thought and action by finding the new premises so quickly, did not prove themselves so clever over the subsequent arrangements they made. The reason for this may have been the fact that everything had of necessity to be planned in such a rush, and therefore the finer details suffered in consequence. One vast exercising yard was provided, the Committee doubtless having rosy ideas of their canine charges romping about in what would represent comparative freedom, in happy contrast to the restrictions of the inadequate space at Holloway that had hitherto been available. What did in fact happen was that, once released from the confines of their pens and let loose in this yard, the dogs all went crazy, leaping about, barking and fighting, and completely out of control. When it became time for them to be gathered together and returned to their pens to allow the next batch of dogs to have their turn, it took the poor kennelmen a long time to round up their charges. The dogs, of course, were thoroughly enjoying the whole performance, thinking that it was laid on especially for their entertainment. By the time the last one had been rounded up and the door of the final pen slammed shut, the patience of the kennelmen was well nigh exhausted, and language was flying around that would certainly have startled the lady members of the committee. Judging by early photographs, that first group of kennelmen were all heavyweights with figures that did not lend themselves to violent exercise.

So the most imperative task was to divide up the exercising yard into manageable areas; it was realised that the sexes would have to be kept apart. It was also found expedient to separate the larger dogs from the smaller ones to prevent intimidation and bullying by either size. Shelters also had to be built in the exercising yards to provide some degree of protection from the more extreme elements.

All sorts of small innovations were made that helped with the smoother daily running of the Home, and a pattern was formed, which has been followed to this day, whereby the general maintenance of the Home is carried out by the staff wherever possible, calling in professionals only when absolutely necessary.

Financial problems were bound to continue and, shortly after the move had been made, the Committee found themselves obliged to go to the moneylenders. This is not surprising, as the Holloway premises remained unsold and the new buildings had to be paid for. With creditors beginning to be pressing, what was in those days the enormous sum of £4,000 was borrowed at the then exorbitant rate of interest of 10% per annum from the British Mutual Society.

It looks as if the Committee were involving themselves in very tricky—and what might have turned out to be somewhat dubious—financial negotiations. The original loan they had had from the London and Westminster Bank had, as we know, been made on the security of the land at Hollinworth Street, and it was backed also by a collateral promissory note signed by five male members of the Committee. Now, less than a year later, here they were borrowing a further sum from a different source on the same security. It is possible, and more than probable, that they intended repaying the Bank loan with this fresh sum of money.

The sale of the Holloway property was hanging fire, and it remained on their hands for three years, no doubt getting more and more run down and delapidated, as property does when it is empty and therefore neglected. At long last a buyer was found, and it was sold for the knock-down price of £900, which represented a loss of £200 on the land alone, not counting all the improvements that had been made. When we learn that the buyer was none other than Mr James Johnson, the original Superintendent of the Home at Holloway, whose title had recently been changed to that of Manager, and was later to become Secretary, it is hard to believe that he did not withhold from the ears of the Committee offers for the property that came to him direct. By doing this, the asking price would come down, and so he was able to move in and make a very profitable transaction for himself, at the expense of the Home.

James Johnson, it would seem, held the Committee in the palm of his hand, for they found themselves obliged to borrow a further £100 from him, adding to their other substantial debts, towards the £2,000 that they had to pay to the British Mutual Society before that investment company would release the Hollinworth Street deeds.

Mercifully, an unexpected windfall fell into their laps just at the time when they needed it most in the form of a legacy of £1,000 from Mrs Hambleton, who had been the first to open the

48

original subscription list with a donation of two guineas. The necessary sum of money was therefore made up, and the sale of their white elephant was able to go through; something which must have lifted a great burden of worry off the shoulders of the male members of the Committee, who had made themselves responsible for the debts incurred by the Home.

These men appear to have been well-meaning but comparatively unversed in business matters. It was fortunate that in 1876 a Miss Lloyd, herself a member of the Committee, offered to take over the mortgage on the Battersea property from the investment company. What is more, she asked for only 5% interest per annum, half of the rate that had been paid for the previous five years. At the same time another fortuitous legacy of £800 arrived to swell the coffers of the Home, thus enabling the outstanding debt to be reduced to £1,200.

The mid-1870s were to prove times of trouble for the Committee in many ways. In 1875 the first question was raised in the courts of the rights of a purchaser to a dog from the Home. Although it was clearly stated in the Act of 1867 that dogs that had been kept for three days, should then become the absolute property of the Police or that of their Agents, in which capacity the Home had acted ever since the negotiation of the first contracts, several cases were brought challenging those rights.

In that same year, 1875, the first rumours were heard that dogs were taken to the Home only to be re-sold for the purposes of vivisection. Nothing could have been further from the truth— and certainly nothing could have been less likely when it is borne in mind on what tenets the Home had originally been founded and the acute sensitivity towards the suffering of animals felt by all the people concerned with the running of the Home. So widespread and vicious were these rumours that eventually the Committee felt obliged to take their problem to the police, who immediately recommended an investigator, to be employed by the Committee, who would go thoroughly into the allegations.

After several weeks of what must have been exhaustive research the detective, Mr Limeburn, was able to report that the rumours were totally unfounded, and that no dog at any time had been taken from the Home for the purposes of vivisection. In the light of what happened regarding dogstealing a few years later, it is possible, of course, that dogs may have ended up at the hospitals for the purposes of vivisection, but this would have been quite outside the knowledge of the Committee.

Limeburn's published report, however, did not succeed in quietening the rumours, and snide whispers persisted constantly during the ensuing twenty-five years, and then intermittently right down to the present day.

It would have been absurd for an institution set up to alleviate suffering among dogs to have connived in such practices—practices that were totally abhorred by all the members of the Committee. One of the firmest principles on which the Home was founded, and one that has been strictly adhered to ever since, was that no animal would, with the knowledge of the Committee, end up on the vivisectionist's table, nor indeed, be used for experiments of any kind.

To implement this principle, every Annual Report issued by the Home carries the following paragraph:

> Each purchaser is required to sign a form absolving the Committee from all responsibility with regard to the dog, stating the purpose for which the animal is required, *undertaking that it shall not be used for the purposes or vivisection*, nor as a performing dog, *and further stating that he is not a dealer nor the agent of a dealer.*

Back in 1868, before the removal to Battersea, a written application had been received from a Mr Murphy, resident surgeon at the Royal Free Hospital, asking that he should be supplied with dogs from the Home for his experiments. The Committee were horrified, and an inspector was immediately despatched by the Secretary of the RSPCA, Mr John Colam, who was also a member of the Committee of the Dogs' Home, to explain to Mr Murphy in person exactly what the feeling of the Committee on the subject of vivisection was, and acquainting him with fact that it would therefore be totally impossible for him to acquire dogs for his purpose from the Home.

John Colam of the RSPCA was an outstanding character, for not only was he Secretary of that body, and editor of the official mouthpiece of the society, *Animal World*, but he was also one of the founder members of the National Society for the Prevention of Cruelty to Children. As a young man he had been one of the

Whittington Lodge, designed as a cats' home

The Home after the offices had first been rebuilt

A queue for the first free veterinary clinic

All the dogs were given a thorough inspection on arrival at the Home

prime movers in the abolition of the cruel sport of cock fighting, and in 1870 he was instrumental in nipping in the bud an attempt that was made to introduce and establish bull-fighting as a spectator sport in this country.

Early that year advertisements started to appear on hoardings around London heralding 'A Grand Spanish Entertainment of Bull Fighters' to be held in the Agricultural Hall at Islington, the mecca of many spectacular events. These posters evidently served their purpose, catching the imagination of the general public, for on the appointed night the arena was full to capacity. A thrilling entertainment had been mounted, and a hush of expectancy had spread over the place as the fourth bull of the evening was about to be pierced with an arrow.

Suddenly the spell was broken as the lithe figure of a young man was seen leaping over the barrier, followed closely by a group of policemen in true Victorian melodramatic style.

At first the tightly packed audience could not make out what was happening, and probably thought that this must be a thief trying to escape from the police. However, the truth suddenly dawned on them that this was in fact someone who was out to spoil their evening's fun. The breathless hush ended abruptly as the air was filled with piercing whistles and catcalls, quickly followed by an ugly rush of angry spectators into the arena itself.

The agile young man who had leapt the barrier and brought the wrath of the crowd on his head was none other than John Colam, bent on doing his duty as Secretary of the RSPCA, the body that had been set up to prevent cruelty to animals. Although he was knocked hither and thither by the angry crowd, he stood his ground firmly and courageously, until at last the police were able to persuade him that he must beat a strategic retreat to avoid what looked very like turning into the lynching of a man rather than the piercing of an animal.

He spent the next couple of weeks in bed, nursing his bruises and contusions, but happy in the knowledge that by his swift, if somewhat foolhardy, action he had certainly put an end to any prospect of bull-fighting becoming a national sport. He was treated as a hero by animal lovers from all over the country, and a few weeks later was presented with a silver goblet bearing an account of the incident in elaborate lettering on its side.

To return to the Dogs' Home. More trouble was on its way. In 1877 the police found themselves obliged to put out a general order to say that, owing to the number of complaints they were receiving daily about dangerous dogs at large in suburban areas, all dogs henceforth found wandering unattended within the Metropolitan Police District would be seized forthwith. However, before putting this order into action they did have the courtesy to approach the Committee of the Dogs' Home to ask for their co-operation in the handling of the overwhelmingly large numbers of dogs that would certainly be brought in.

This police order was the forerunner of several, and provided the first intimation of the great rabies scare that was soon to sweep the country, bringing untold suffering to countless perfectly healthy animals in its wake. The rabies scare caused a panic that led to scenes of appalling brutality, for, while they were under orders to destroy forthwith any dog suspected of being rabid, the police were not permitted to carry poisons, firearms or knives. This meant that they had to resort to using their truncheons to bludgeon the poor creatures to death, leading to horrifying scenes as they carried out their brutal task, watched and encouraged with savage glee by the vicious crowds that always seem to materialise from thin air to witness any scenes of violence.

A letter was immediately sent to the newspapers from the Dogs' Home in an attempt to inform the general public of the true facts regarding rabies. An extract from their letter serves to illustrate what was happening all over London, when many of the so-called 'confirmed' cases of rabies were nothing more than attacks of hysteria, or possibly epilepsy:

Ignorance of the real symptoms of rabies will inevitably lead to atrocities in our streets. A fit is not a symptom, as is popularly supposed, and no alarm ought to be felt by the public when they see a convulsed dog in the street. Unfortunately, people do not stop to reason, but give way to their fears, when they see such an occurrence, and the poor brute is consequently driven up one street and down another at the utmost speed, kicked, stoned, terrorised and maddened into fury, until he bites someone obstructing or pursuing him, whereupon without further evidence he is pronounced mad . . . A few days ago, as a policeman was bringing in a half-breed homeless pug to Battersea, the animal had a fit in a street adjacent to the Home. The cry was set up—'Kill him, he is mad.' 'Knock his brains out.' 'If he bites you, you are a dead man,' etc. Fortunately the dog was taken up by one of our keepers, whose experience enabled him to make a correct diagnosis of the dog's complaint. The dog was brought to the Home where medicine was administered and kindness bestowed upon him. It soon recovered and was subsequently sent to a good home and a kind mistress.

It was only natural, though, that feelings should run high, for ignorance was rife, and hysteria on such a burning subject is extremely contagious. It is only too easy to imagine anyone panicking when faced with what appears at first sight to be a rabid dog, knowing the dire consequences of even a touch from its saliva on the tiniest abrasion of the skin.

Several years later, in 1886, at a time when there had been sixty confirmed cases of rabies detected during the year in the Dogs' Home, an appalling story hit the headlines of the newspapers. To become known as the 'Baker Street Mad Dog Case', it was the subject of two court actions, and was brought to the attention of the Queen herself. The Queen was known to be worried about the brutalising effect that the implementation of the Police Orders and Muzzling Orders were having on the police force in general, as is evidenced by a telegram handed in at Perth on 27 May 1886, addressed to her Private Secretary, Sir Henry Ponsonby at St James Palace:[1]

'Read last night St James about dogs and lost order I protest vehemently against such tyranny and cruelty beautiful weather　　　　　　　　　　　　　　　　　　The Queen'

The Baker Street Mad Dog Case concerned a spaniel, and resulted in a lady called Miss Revell being sued for assault against a police officer in the course of his duties. In spite of her declaration of provocation, the findings were against her, and she was fined twenty shillings with two shillings costs—although the magistrate who heard the case did have the grace to add that Miss Revell had some excuse, as she was excited at the time.

An extract from a letter she and some friends wrote to *The Spectator* (a copy of which they sent to Queen Victoria), which was published on 24 July 1886, will serve to explain the reason for her so-called 'excitement'.

. . . The dog was in perfect health, and had slept as usual on the bed of the servant, whose witness was given against the police in the Marylebone Police-court. Both she and her mistress positively state that at half-past 8 the spaniel accompanied the former to the lady's bedroom, that being the hour at which it was customary to 'call' her, and to carry in the morning cup of tea. While the lady drank her tea, the spaniel lay upon her bed and she caressed it. The dog was then taken away by the servant, who gave it its breakfast as usual, muzzled it, and turned it out into the street, the landlord objecting to its presence in the back-yard of the house. It is not known exactly how long the spaniel remained outside, but, unfortunately, some holiday-making street-boys espied it and teased it. Its muzzle thus became disarranged, and a lady—who signs this letter—seeing the dog from her window, and observing that its muzzle was twisted and seemed to be hurting it, came out of her house to put it straight, and patted the dog. This incident alone suffices to show that the little animal exhibited no symptoms of rabidity. Yet the police aver that a gentleman who happened to be passing at the time, and to whom Miss Footner [who was evidently the lady from the opposite house] spoke, went on to the police-station and informed the constables that there was a 'stray mad dog in Baker Street'. This gentleman, however, has not been identified. When the police arrived on the scene, Miss Footner had returned to her house, and the dog was lying on the steps of No 9 from whence they drove him to No 49, and there flung a lassoo over him. In this house Miss Revell, the chief witness against the police, was then staying. She, knowing the dog by sight, came to the door, intending to tell the constables that it belonged to a lady at No 8, and was not a 'lost dog', as they seemed to suppose. For her belief then was that the police wished to secure the dog in order to take it to the 'Home' at Battersea. As she went to the door, however, she heard the first 'thud' of the truncheon on the poor creature's spine, and a piteous cry. She opened the door instantly, and asked Inspector Prendergast what he was doing. He replied that they were killing a 'mad' dog. Miss Revell protested that the dog was not mad, and begged to be allowed to take it into her house. The constables became very insolent, and the Inspector, addressing one of them—149 D—said, 'If she likes it, give the dog another before her, and let her see it!' The dog was then struck again and again on the spine and on the nose, Miss Revell continuing to remonstrate. Finding that all she said was unavailing, she went back into the house, sat down on the stairs, and cried; but presently, unable to bear the horrible and continual sounds of the blows, and the heartrending moans and shrieks of the poor dying beast, she again went out, and this time used very warm language to the Inspector. Even yet the dog was not dead, and being angrily repulsed by the constables, she ran upstairs in a frenzy of horror and indignation, seized a pitcher full of water, and emptied it over the policemen. For this act she was subsequently summoned, and fined (the amount, with costs, being £8.8s.). Some of the witnesses assert that the dog was being beaten to death for three-quarters of an hour, crying all the time, others say half-an-hour; but the lowest computation is twenty minutes. A great crowd collected, and a boy, passing with his father, was so shocked at the horrible spectacle that he swooned. A lady sent her servant from a neighbouring house to offer a sovereign to buy the dog, and the Inspector, it is asserted, swore at the girl. After the constables had done their worst, the poor little animal, still breathing, and covered with wounds, was strapped on a water-cart and removed, 'to be finished at the station'.

The letter went on to state that the dog had an alibi when assertions were made by police witnesses that it had been seen on the streets at 7.30am, and it finished with a very cogent paragraph:

How long is this ridiculous tyranny, and the still more ridiculous panic which initiated it, to continue? 'Mad' dogs have been as plentiful as blackberries since the exploits of

M. Pasteur and the extraordinary statistics emanating from the Rue d'Ulm have been made public. Perhaps the craze will wear itself out in time; but meanwhile, private property, to say nothing of human feelings, ought to be protected from organised outrage in the manner just described; *and measures should be at once taken to reinstate the police in the respect and confidence of the public . ...*

Read nearly a hundred years later, the whole letter carries the ring of truth, but it is the last few words (my italics) that lend authority to the whole statement, and give the certain feeling that it was written by responsible and thinking people. It makes one wonder exactly what did go on in that Police Court, or what evasive actions were taken to cover up the true facts.

Queen Victoria was so sickened and horrified on reading this tragic and terrible account, that she demanded an immediate and full enquiry at the highest level.

Her Private Secretary, Sir Henry Ponsonby, was asked to write two letters, the first to Miss Revell:[2]

Her Majesty cannot sufficiently express her horror at the statements so frequently made in the newspaper of cruelty inflicted on dumb creatures especially on dogs 'Man's best friends' . . . The Queen has asked for a report on the case to which you refer . . .

It is, however, interesting to note that on the copy of this letter which is filed in the Royal Archives, after 'Man's best friends' were originally the words: 'though it must be added that many of these stories do not bear the test of investigation'. These have been deleted, the following being substituted: 'The Queen has desired me to forward your letter to the Secretary of State for the Home Department, with a request that he will enquire into the circumstances of the case which you have communicated to Her Majesty.'

Sir Henry's second letter was written to the then Home Secretary, Sir Godfrey Lushington, and he received the following reply dated 30 July 1886:[3]

Dear Sir H. Ponsonby, The case to which you refer of alleged cruelty by the Police towards a dog has already been investigated in the most efficient manner open to the Home Office; that is by a Police Magistrate. The case was tried out in open Court, each party had full opportunity to give evidence, and that evidence was tested by cross examination. The result as you will see from the enclosed print was that the charges of cruelty against the Police were dismissed, and those who preferred them had to pay £4.4s. in each case. This seems conclusive.

I also forward to you some observations which I have received from the Commissioner of Police. I am certain he is anxious that these necessary Regulations shall be carried out by the police so as to occasion as little suffering as possible. Yours very truly, Godfrey Lushington.

The letter of the Commissioner of Police, Sir Charles Warren, to the Home Secretary had been as follows:[4]

Dear Mr Lushington, I return you the letter to Her Majesty which you have sent me for any observations. I have only to observe that it is bristling with false statements and exaggerations.

The following remarks may be useful:

1. I wrote on hearing of the Charge to urge the Society for Prevention of Cruelty to Animals to take up the case. The Secretary replied that any action for cruelty would fail.

2. I sent the carcase of the dog to the Dogs' Home for *post mortem* examination. The Secretary neglected to have it examined and hence this prevents the Police constable proving that the dog was mad.

3. Great pressure has been centred in this case to injure the officers who risked their lives to protect the public. One lady offered the SPCA a sum of £5 if they would obtain the dismissal of the officers.

4. I forward a copy of the observation of the Magistrate.

5. A dog may be healthy at one time of day and in a dangerous condition at another. During the last 20 days we have had two cases in which dogs led by their owners have suddenly become mad and their owners have requested the Police to kill the dogs.

6. 56 dogs have been killed in the streets in the last 25

days—of these 16 were rabid and the remainder mostly suffering from epilepsy and dangerous to the public.

7. I enclose a return of dogs killed in the week ending 10 July.

8. I enclose a copy of a letter about a child bitten by a dog.

9. There has been so much malice shown in the manner in which certain persons have endeavoured to break down and injure the police constables who killed the dog—that it will be a good thing if the matter can be further exposed. Truly yours, Charles Warren.

That had to be the end of it as far as the Palace was concerned, but Sir Charles Warren was finding himself increasingly the subject of much abuse from people who were horrified at the conditions prevailing at the time, and an open letter to him, written on entirely satirical lines, in reply to a letter Sir Charles had himself written to *The Times*, was published that September, a copy being kept among Queen Victoria's papers.

Headed 'The Dog Regulations' it was addressed personally to Sir Charles Warren at Scotland Yard.[5]

Sir, All men who duly appreciate the dignity of human-nature, and the sacredness of human-life, will applaud to the echo your noble, merciful, and sagacious opinion which appears in 'The Times' Newspaper of yesterday's date. Your sentiment as reported there, being—'*I am of opinion that the life of one human being is of more importance than all the Dogs in Christendom.*' The sentence is most admirable—it ought to be written in letters of gold!

But, why halt where you do? why not say—'The life of one human being (no matter whose) is of more importance than all the Dogs, Horses, Camels, &c., &c., in Christendom?' Why stop at the Dogs? Why not say, 'than all the animals?'

And, why confine yourself to 'Christendom', and leave out the rest of the World and all other religious beliefs? Don't, I beg, 'make *two* bites at a cherry'. 'Go the whole animal'. 'Out-Herod Herod'. Those weak-minded men and silly women who like Dogs will of course cry out against you—but never mind them. They will bring against your noble sentiment, the opinion of Byron,

The poor dog, in life the firmest friend,
The first to welcome, foremost to defend.

And they will quote Sir Walter Scott's assertion, that 'The dog is the friend of man, except where man justly incurs his enmity'. Also, Robert Burns will be quoted, where he says 'The dog puts the Christian to shame'. But, my dear Sir Charles, regard them not, for what did Byron, Scott and Burns know about the Canine Race and Human Race, and what their comparative values are? Nothing, absolutely nothing, compared to your knowledge. There is, there can be, there shall be no doubt that the life of the basest wretch, the most atrocious miscreant that your Department—that the London Police—ever brought to Justice, is worth the lives of Landseer's Distinguished Member of the Humane Society, The Dogs of St Bernard, The Shepherd's Chief Mourner, Grey-Friars Bobby, and all the dogs who bravely saved human life at the risk of their own, or faithfully solaced the sufferings of the poor and lonely.

Your Department well remembers the late Mr Peace* (fortunately for honest folk now '*at* Peace'). Well, these dog-loving, dog-owning fools and fanatics will boldly assert that one honest watch-dog is of more importance than a universe of Peaces. But *we* know better, Sir Charles. Rascal, thief, burglar, and murderer out-value all the dog in Christendom.

'Let Gallows gape for Dog, let Man go free'.

Go ahead, say I. Down with the Dogs. I admire the style in which you butcher them in the streets of pious London. Do all your men like the work though? Some may think that the guardians of the law ought not to be forced to do knackers' work—they may consider it brutal and degrading to manly minds. Some of the Constabulary, no doubt, are fond of animals. However, most fortunately, their

---

* It is interesting to relate that Charlie Peace, the notorious burglar and murderer, was always accompanied by a dog when he went about his nefarious deeds, this dog acting as a look-out and giving warning of anyone's approach. On Peace's final arrest and subsequent execution, that dog was taken to the Dogs' Home at Battersea where it acted as a watch-dog until the end of its days.

Head is above such weak-mindedness, and would mass-
acre all the dogs in Christendom rather than a Mr Peace or
the Netherby Hall murderers should receive one bite . . .

Sir Charles Warren resigned shortly afterwards but, however
unpopular the Muzzling Acts and Police Orders were, it is a
fact that they did succeed in making some sort of order out of
the chaos that existed, eventually putting the situation under
some sort of control. The numbers of cases in the country of
rabies fell to only 38 by 1892, although they were to increase
dramatically to 727 in 1895 when the Police tried what was to
prove a rather disastrous experiment, turning over control to
the local authorities. Finally even firmer measures were taken
and the disease was eventually eradicated from this country
when the stringent quarantine controls were introduced in
1902, with only an occasional outbreak thereafter.

5 Establishment and Success

It is now necessary to go back a few years in the history of the Dogs' Home, to 1880, when a constant 18,000 dogs were passing through it each year; by this time it had already achieved world-wide reknown.

James Johnson had died in 1877, carrying with him to his grave the secret of the Holloway affair, and his successor was an ex-RSPCA superintendent called Thomas Scoborio. He, however, stayed in the post for only six years, until 1883, before tendering his resignation. It looks as if he was in fact asked to go, for, when making a new appointment, the Committee announced that a new code of bye-laws had been drawn up for the management of the Home, the enforcement of which by an intelligent, practical and, above all, *humane* superior officer would offer the best guarantee that their Institution deserved the support of the public.

In the early years, family connections were destined to play an important part not only in the shaping of the policy of the Home, but also in its day-to-day running. At about the time of Thomas Scoborio's resignation James Pavitt, the first keeper, who had served the Home so well and faithfully from the time of its inception at Holloway twenty-one years before, died. His place as Head Keeper was taken by George Tagg, who had come to Holloway as his assistant and had shortly afterwards married Pavitt's only daughter, Rosa, who was then working as a clerk in the office of the Home.

Scoborio's successor as Secretary was Charles Colam, son of John Colam who had been a member of the Committee for several years, and about whose exploits in his early years as Secretary of the RSPCA we have already heard. This appointment was to make an even stronger bond between the Dogs' Home and the RSPCA, the aims of which societies having always run on parallel lines.

The first intimation of royal interest in the Home had been, received back in 1879, when word was received from Buckingham Palace that the Prince of Wales was proposing to make a visit to the Home at Battersea, bringing with him Queen Marie of Belgium. The news of this prospective Royal visit naturally brought great excitement to the Home, and a spate of white-washing, painting and scrubbing was feverishly begun. This royal visit, like so many others all over the world, doubtless provided both the spur and the incentive for several pressing jobs of maintenance to be carried out in double-quick time.

It is evident that all was in apple-pie order by the time that the Prince arrived with his royal guest, for, after making a minute and detailed inspection of the premises, they took their leave of the then Secretary, Mr Scoborio, congratulating him warmly on the working and general management of the Home.

1883 was a year that saw not only a new Secretary and a new Superintendent, but also the setting-up of a subcommittee to look into the possible expansion of the Home. This fact is difficult to relate to the interest-free loan of £1,000 that they received that same year from the RSPCA, although that loan may not have been received until after the findings of the subcommittee were published.

Their report recommended that the idea of once more taking dogs as boarders should be abandoned, but that an improved entrance should be made and a home for cats be built. It is amusing to note that the suggestion that a house should be built for the Secretary came last in the list of recommendations.

1883 was a year that seems to have marked a vital turning-point in the fortunes of the Home, and it saw another royal visitor; this time it was Queen Victoria's youngest son, Prince Leopold, Duke of Albany.

In 1882, the year before his visit to the Dogs' Home, he married Princess Helen, the daughter of the reigning Prince of Waldeck and Pyrmont, and sister to the then Queen of the Netherlands. The young couple had a little daughter who had been born on 25 February 1883, Princess Alice who, when she grew up, married Prince Alexander of Teck, brother of Queen Mary, who was later created the 1st Earl of Athlone.

This baby girl, therefore, was only a few weeks old at the time of her father's visit to Battersea, and it is likely that the little terrier the Prince took home with him in his carriage was the dog that Princess Alice remembers in her nursery. Its name was Skippy, and it was her constant companion, as is shown by the charming picture of her taken at the age of three, with hat, gloves, button boots and brolly, the little dog sitting alertly at her side.

Prince Leopold made as thorough an inspection of the Home as that made by his eldest brother, four years earlier, and on his return to the Palace he evidently gave the Queen a glowing account of his visit. Only a few months after Prince Leopold's tragically early death the following year, Sir Henry Ponsonby was asked by Her Majesty to pay a visit to the Dogs' Home and to report back to her on what he found.

Queen Victoria, as we have learnt, was deeply interested in the welfare of all animals, but particularly of dogs, to which animals she invariably referred as 'Man's best friend'. She had many dogs at Windsor to whom she was much attached, and used to erect memorials to her special favourites. From these we learn that she had dachshunds there in her early married life, long before they were known to the general public of either England or Germany. In those days they were used for sport only by the nobility of Germany and Austria. On the slopes in the Windsor Home Park is an elaborate monument to a dachshund which takes the form of a marble pillar on a plinth of granite, and bears the inscription: 'Here is buried Deckel, the faithful German Dachshund of Queen Victoria, who brought him from Coburg in 1845. Died August 10, 1859. Aged 15 years.'

Sir Henry Ponsonby, therefore, came to Battersea and made a searching tour, delving into every nook and cranny with the military eye for detail that is evidenced when we read the papers he prepared daily for the Queen, ever mindful of her constant desire to be fully and completely informed about those affairs in which at that moment she was taking an interest. However, in spite of all his meticulous inspection, the Queen was evidently not entirely satisfied with his report, for he soon returned to have a further look—presumably at something about which the Queen wished to be further informed. On his return to the Palace the second time he must have found himself able to answer all Her Majesty's searching questions adequately, for on 22 December 1885, in one of her frequent memoranda to her Private Secretary, she asked him to send a donation to the Home, and also to indicate to the Committee that she would like to send a similar sum each ensuing year.[6]

Sir Henry acted promptly, for he replied to the Queen the next day, saying that he had already sent a sum of money to the Home, and had informed the Secretary that she would like to give a similar amount each year. Sir Henry was evidently a past master at looking after the interests of his Royal employer, for he added that, as Her Majesty had mentioned two figures, he had chosen the lower one, since that meant that the donation could always be increased in the future.

So the report of the twenty-fifth Annual Meeting of the Dogs' Home was able to begin with the following words read by Charles Colam:

> In meeting you here to-day your Committee welcome you with more than ordinary pleasure, as the 25th Annual Report contains the encouraging announcement that Her Majesty the Queen has graciously bestowed on your Institution the distinguished honour of her patronage by a donation of £10, and by a request that her name may be enrolled as an annual subscriber of a like amount to your funds.

Then followed a superbly fulsome speech by the Chairman of the Committee, George Measom, JP, who was a man of many parts and evidently an extremely likeable character. Not only did he become Chairman of the RSPCA and Chairman of the Cancer Hospital, but also, under a pseudonym, he was well known as a successful writer of adventure books for boys.

> . . . Last year we expressed our satisfactions at the important fact that HRH The Prince of Wales had become one of our subscribers. (*Cheers.*) This year we are in a position to state that Her Most Gracious Majesty the Queen has not only sent a donation but has kindly added her name to the list of subscribers for £10 per annum. (*Loud Cheers.*) . . . As the arm of justice we are told is long enough to reach the wrongdoer, so the tender heart of our beloved Queen goes out towards suffering whether felt by man or beast. (*Cheers.*)

Mr Measom was evidently completely carried away by then, for he continued:

It is almost impossible to speak without a feeling of emotion concerning the Queen of these realms. Every day some fresh instance occurs of her goodness, not only to her people but when within her power to all created things in the United Kingdom. Very shortly we shall, for it is within measurable distance, have to celebrate the jubilee or fiftieth year of her reign, and then from every Legislative Assembly, every learned society, every church and chapel, and every charitable institution in this country, in India, in Burmah, in Australia, in New Zealand, in Fiji and other remote places, one prayer of heartfelt thanks will go up to the Giver of all good for having spared the valuable life of Her Majesty the Queen and enabled her to exercise her beneficent rule over more than one fifth of the great family of man; and that for such a long period. (*Loud cheers.*)

After this meeting, a studiedly careful letter was drafted and sent on behalf of the Committee to Sir Henry Ponsonby in which it was asked if the Queen would be gracious enough to grant her patronage to the Home, pointing out that patronage had already been granted by both her sons who had visited it.

This request was passed on immediately to Queen Victoria, who wrote diagonally across the top of Sir Henry's note, underlining some of the words several times: 'Most certainly. No one loves Dogs more than The Queen or would wish to do more to promote their comfort and happiness. They are Man's truest friends.'[7]

When sending her first donation, the Queen had also made the suggestion that dogs should be kept not only for the three days then required by law but perhaps for up to ten. Lord Onslow, the second President of the Home, who had succeeded Marquess Townshend and was later Governor of New Zealand, wrote post haste from Clandon Park, his country home, to explain that in accordance with this request, the Committee had extended the time from three to five days, but he added that, as the first and last days of a dog's stay at the Home were not counted, they were kept for virtually a week.[8]

There is no doubt at all that the warm-hearted Queen gave

deep and constant thought to the welfare and ultimate fate of 'her beloved dogs', as is fully evidenced by note after note addressed by her to Sir Henry Ponsonby in which she expresses the deepest concern for them. However, this extension of time that the dogs had to be kept added enormously to the pressures placed on the Home during that year in every way, both financially and practically. The Police Order for the seizure of all unmuzzled dogs, coupled with the fact that Colonel Sir Edmund Henderson, the then Commissioner of the Metropolitan Police who was to be succeeded shortly by the unpopular Sir Charles Warren, had, without notice, extended the area that was to be covered by the Dogs' Home. Originally it had covered a six-mile radius from Charing Cross, and now this radius was to be doubled, quadrupling the total area concerned, making about 450 square miles in all. This led to the highest intake of dogs in the entire history of the Home. 35,064 dogs were handled in the year, with some 500 being brought in on one single day, meaning that there were 750 dogs in the Home at one time. Conditions were chaotic, and the situation was only slightly relieved by the hasty rental and conversion into extra emergency kennel space of two more railway arches from the London, Dover and Chatham Railway.

With such enormous numbers of dogs passing through the Home, it is not surprising that the subject of their painless destruction had been raised at the outset of the great rabies scare. In 1882–3 the subcommittee that was looking into the possible extensions and improvements to the Home as a whole also made a recommendation that there should be provision for a chamber for the painless destruction of both dogs and cats, and particularly of the latter. The administration of the death-dealing drops of prussic acid to a dog was a hazardous enough business, but administering them to cats was almost impossible when faced with a cat's sharp claws and needle-like teeth. Dogs had always been found to be far more passive subjects, and were moderately easy to handle by the experienced and highly skilled men who carried out this unenviable task, developing an amazing degree of dexterity in their work. The subcommittee pointed out that the effects of prussic acid, although providing an almost instantaneous death, were certainly far from painless, and it was disposed to think that

One policeman brought in more than a thousand strays

Dogs were used with great success to collect for the Home at mainline stations

Dogs recruited from the Home 'somewhere in England' during the last war

Battersea should follow the lead taken by homes in the United States of America, where highly successful lethal chambers were already in daily use.

It is evident that public opinion was already swinging towards this new innovation, for around about the same time both the *Daily Telegraph* and the *Pall Mall Gazette* carried simultaneous articles suggesting that a lethal chamber would prove a most necessary adjunct to the Dogs' Home on the twin grounds of utility and humanity.

The funds to put such a scheme into action were offered by Mr Richard Barlow Kennet, who had earlier made a handsome donation to enable a cat house to be built: the work for this had already been started.

As far back as 1869, Dr Benjamin Ward Richardson, who was to gain international repute for his work on anaesthetics, then a comparatively new and much needed branch of medicine, had suggested to the RSPCA that the use of a narcotic would provide a suitable means of painless destruction for domestic animals. While still a student at St Andrews University in Scotland, Dr Richardson had in the late 1840s started experimenting with the common puff-ball, as it was then common practice in country districts to collect these puff-balls and to burn them in order to stupefy bees when taking their honey from the hive. Later on, while still a student, Sir Benjamin was present at an operation performed under the influence of chloroform. As he watched the patient drift away in happy oblivion as to what was taking place—indeed, so much so that she nearly died from the effects of the chloroform and not from the surgery—the fact occurred to Richardson that this would surely be a well-nigh perfect way of despatching domestic animals. In later years he set up a lethal chamber in the garden of his home at Mortlake in Surrey, which he made available to his neighbours for the painless destruction of their pets.

On reading the report of the Battersea sub-committee, Dr Richardson offered his services to the Home, and designed a lethal chamber. It was a long cage on wheels into which from ten to fifty dogs could be put at any one time. This cage was then run into a lethal chamber where carbonic acid gas through which chloroform was introduced in the form of a spray was then pumped into the cage. Half an hour later, the cage was withdrawn, and the carcases removed. Death was caused by an overdose of anaesthetic, and not by suffocation or asphyxia as was feared by many people.

A contemporary journalist wrote a vivid and haunting description of the process:

> There was a silence of about a minute, after which began a strange, unearthly wailing cry—just like the sound of some discordant crowd heard in the far distance. It would be easy to convince yourself that it is a cry of anguish and despair and piteous suffering. The fact is, however, that chloroform is an important element of the air of the chamber, and the dogs are just falling under the influence of it. Medical men recognise in this doleful wailing cry merely the same effect that chloroform always has upon human beings . . . There is a steady crescendo and then an equally steady diminuendo, and in about another minute all is over.
>
> Doggie's troubles are all at an end, and his faithless friends are all forgotten. The biter and the bitten are slumbering side by side in peace and amity never to be broken again.

The introduction of a lethal chamber, combined with the fact that so many animals were having to be destroyed, presented the Committee with even further problems; these were, not unnaturally, concerned with the ultimate disposal of the bodies.

Up to that date, the carcasses had been taken to a farm at Enfield, on the borders of London, in Essex, where they were allowed to decompose and then used for manure. However, people living nearby were starting to complain of the smell, and the farmer concerned was understandably refusing to take any more loads, so it was becoming urgently necessary for the Home to make alternative arrangements. Rather on the spur of the moment, the decision was made to build a crematorium which it was hoped would deal quickly and cleanly with the distasteful job.

Perhaps rather misguidedly, the Committee felt that their new Patron, the Queen, should be made aware of their proposed crematorium.[9] They soon found their mistake when they received an abrupt reply to the letter in which they had told Sir Henry Ponsonby that this new method was being introduced as a sanitary measure. Sir Henry's answer said abruptly that the Queen was decidedly opposed to the burning of the bodies of dogs;[10] in a further letter, written the next day,[11] he told them that the Queen was informed that quicklime thrown over the bodies when they were buried prevented any evil consequence.

Poor Charles Colam, the Secretary of the Home, found himself in a great dilemma, for the last thing he wanted to do, especially as a comparative newcomer to the job, was to offend his Monarch. He hastily wrote again to Sir Henry pointing out the obvious facts—in the first place how difficult it would be to find a burial ground that would be large enough to accommodate all the carcasses, and stressing that it would prove an expensive operation quite beyond the resources of the Home. He also added, no doubt hoping to ameliorate the situation by showing prudent economy, that the Committee considered that they would not be acting either responsibly or correctly if they spent the Home's money on work of an impermanent nature.[12]

The reply from the Palace to his letter came promptly as usual, and stated that the Queen's opinion was unchanged, but though she could not, of course, object to such an arrangement as a crematorium, she would not contribute to it.[13]

It is doubtful whether the Committee had indeed been so naïve as to suppose that the Queen would help with the financing of such a project. All they sought was her approval.

The crematorium was going to cost money, so an appeal was launched, but it brought in only £245, a mere drop in the ocean. However, once more Mr Barlow Kennet came to the rescue with an advance of £1,000, this being a sum of money left in trust to him by his wife who had recently died, for his lifetime, which was destined, on his death, to go eventually to the Home; for this generous loan he charged the Home only 3% interest. So the first crematorium was built at the rear of the Home.

During that same year a malicious, irresponsible and entirely untrue rumour was spread in the newspapers that the Dogs' Home had received a legacy of £10,000. This rumour led to an instant drop in donations at the very time when money was most needed, and two separate loans of £500 each had to be drawn from the Bank, making their total debts in the region of £2,000. An appeal for financial assistance from the general public was immediately mounted, and a request was addressed also to the Government, pointing out the fact that the Home undertook the work of the Police, thus relieving the police funds of heavy calls upon them. This request, however, fell on stony ground and was turned down outright. The following year the Home received its usual £10 from the Metropolitan Police, a sum that had not changed since the first contract had been drawn up in 1868, when the Dogs Act came into being.

6 The End of an Era

The year 1887 saw the Golden Jubilee of Her Majesty, Queen Victoria, and at the Annual General Meeting of the Dogs' Home, George Measom, who was to receive an accolade at the hand of his beloved sovereign three years later, made another of his exaggerated, but highly amusing speeches:

> ... And what of electricity—the future motive power? Three hundred years ago Shakespeare made Ariel say:—'I'll put a girdle round the earth in forty minutes.' What a wonderful foretelling of the electric telegraph! ... All these blessings could not have been carried out except under a stable Government, and we could not have had a stable Government if we had not had a wise Monarch. (*Loud and continued applause.*) I need scarcely add that it is impossible to imagine a ruler who during all those long years has lived so entirely in the affections of her people. Her Majesty's sorrows have always been our sorrows, and ours have been shared by the loving heart of our Queen. May God in His goodness preserve Her Majesty's valuable life for many years. (*Loud Cheers.*)
> I beg to move that a loyal, dutiful and congratulatory address be forwarded to Her Most Gracious Majesty The Queen, Patron of this Institution, in commemoration of the fifty golden years during which Her Majesty has reigned over her people.

In 1888 a grand concert was organised in aid of the Home by what was described as 'a group of like-minded people'. It was held at Grosvenor House, the London home of the Duke of Westminster, who lent it for the occasion, and it raised £420, at a time when every penny was desperately needed.

The list of names of the people concerned with this grand concert is interesting and, although naturally most were theatrical, shows how wide an appeal such an institution as the Dogs' Home had for men and women drawn from all walks of life. They included the actresses Fay Lankester and Ellen Terry, who was at that time in the middle of her triumph at the Lyceum, and Mrs Bancroft, who was the actress Marie Wilton. Others included Lady Dorothy Nevill, who was described by Ellen Terry as 'that distinguished lady of the old school—what a picture of a woman!—was always a fine theatre-goer. Her face always cheered me if I saw it in the theatre, and she was one of the most clever and amusing of the Beefsteak Room guests.' The Beefsteak Room was a room set aside at the Lyceum Theatre as a supper room; it saw a gathering of distinguished people each night. Princess May of Teck, later to be Queen Mary, often visited the Beefsteak Club with her mother, Princess Mary.

At about the same time, the Battersea Committee expressed a debt of gratitude to Mr Yates Carrington, a well-known Victorian animal painter and portraitist, and to the editor of *The Pall Mall Gazette*, who had always been lively to the aims and needs of the Dogs' Home; the two men joined forces to produce a moving article containing an appeal for funds for the Home. This article resulted in donations of £360, and these two sums of money enabled the Committee to pay off the £1,000 to the RSPCA that had been borrowed, interest free, five years before.

The following year, in 1889, a morning performance was given at what was described as 'Terry's Theatre'—this must have been the Lyceum—which the Prince of Wales expressed his intention of gracing with his presence. The play performed was called 'Monte Carlo', and the performers gave their services 'gratuitously', the expression used in the all too brief report of the occasion put out by the Home.

Anti-vivisection, which had always perforce been a subject close to the hearts of the people who served on the Committee, was naturally the main subject chosen by the speaker at the Annual General Meeting in 1891, for he was the Secretary of the London Anti-Vivisection Society, Mr H. J. Reid. He made the first suggestion yet heard that it should be compulsory for all lost dogs in London to be brought to Battersea, for he felt that if this were done then the Home would be bound to become better known and more substantially supported. He was evidently something of a prophet, as this eventually did happen with exactly the results that he had foreseen.

The recently knighted Sir George Measom closed his address at that meeting by reading a poem which he said was to be found in Mrs Suckling's 'Humane Educator':

> *I'm nothing but an ugly dog, whose home is on the street;*
> *I trot along the pavements with my weary muddy feet,*
> *Or crouch aside to envy gallant dogs who flourish by*
> *With dainty jingling collars, and self-complacent eye.*
> *I know my friends—alas, how few!—by some magnetic touch,*
> *Oh, would that all policemen in our town would count as such!*
> *That every star and uniform like mercy's badge might bless*
> *With hope of aid each friendless dog and creature in distress!*
> *And when at last, uncared for, on the stones you see me lie,*
> *Oh! take me to the 'Home', where I painlessly may die!*
> *That 'dying like a dog' may mean no friendless pangs for me,*
> *When life has known but scanty joys, sure, death should gentle be.*

There must surely have been hardly a dry eye in Sir George's audience following that gem of sentiment. Each year the people who attended the Annual General Meeting of the Dogs' Home must have waited anxiously to hear what Sir George was going to produce that afternoon, and they were seldom disappointed.

1891 marked the beginning of the last decade of Queen Victoria's life, and the next year was to see the foundation of the Independent Labour Party, an epoch-making event in the social revolution that was quietly going on in Victorian England. In 1891 elementary education was made absolutely free of charge, and that same year land was bought in the centre of Battersea, intended for a set of municipal buildings. These were completed very quickly, and opened by Lord Rosebery, the first Chairman of the new London County Council, the body that had taken the place of the infamous Metropolitan Board of Works.

In 1893 Sir George Measom produced some novel theories that must have involved him in a good deal of research:

> . . . It is remarkable that from our faithful friend, the dog,

the companion of man, and the guardian of his person and property, should originate so many terms of vile reproach and low comparison as 'you dog', 'you cur', 'you hound', 'you whelp'. According to Horace, the sight of a female dog with young ones was an unlucky omen; and of a sullen discontented person we say that the black dog has walked over him. (*Laughter.*) It is a curious fact that the Australian dog does not bark: and Gardiner in his 'Music of Nature' states that dogs in a state of nature never bark. Sonnini, the Italian Naturalist, speaks of the shepherds' dogs in Egypt not having this faculty; and Columbus found the dogs which he had previously carried to America had lost their propensity for barking. The barking of a dog is an acquired faculty—an effort to speak, which he derives from association with man. To the Israelites the dog was abominable, as shown by the Livitical law. The Egyptians, on the contrary, regarded the dog as an object of adoration; and the Indians looked on it as one of the sacred forms of their deities. To us the dog is not an abomination, neither is he an object of adoration, but he is our dear, good friend, ready at any time and in all places to lay down his life for his master; in return for such love and sacrifice we are called upon at least to protect him from ill-usage, and when his last hour comes, ensure for him a speedy and painless death. (*Cheers.*) No doubt many of you will call to mind those eloquent lines of Longfellow, which express with so much pathos the duty of man and the claims of his dumb fellow creatures:

> *We plead the cause of these dumb mouths*
> *That have no speech.*
> *Only a cry from each to each*
> *In its own kind, with its own laws:*
> *Something that is beyond the reach*
> *of Human power to learn or teach.*

The year after, in 1894, Mrs Suckling's *Humane Educator* again lay on the table in front of Sir George as he stood up to give his annual address, which he finished by picking up the book and reading *Dog and Man* by Henry Downes:

His master's voice was harsh and gruff,
Coarse and hard his hand, but Ruff
Could not worship him enough.

Many a rent the curious eye
In his raiment might descry,
But Ruff could no defect espy.

Of food and drink but little store
Had he; he was old and poor,
But the dog did him adore.

His limbs were weak, his pace was slow,
His friends were gone, his lot was woe,
Humbly behind him Ruff doth go.

Only this one faithful thing
Did unto his fortune cling,
Unto Ruff he was a king:

In 1894 a radical change came about in local government, when the Vicar and churchwardens ceased to be *ex officio* members of the Vestry, and the duties of the old Burial Board, of the Commissioners of Baths and Washhouses, and of the Commissioners of Public Libraries were transferred to the Vestries. This form of local government by Vestry was to continue up to the end of the century, when the Borough Councils came into existence as new administrative bodies elected in an orthodox manner with extended powers.

In 1894, a German called Dr Carl Schneider paid a visit to the Home, and when he returned to Cologne, he published an article which was chosen by Sir George Measom to read at the Annual Meeting the following year:

> ... Any respectable person is allowed to inspect free of charge; a clerk will enter your name and address, and soon you find yourself in a labyrinth of sheds, the inmates of which are asserting themselves to the best of their ability, by barking, howling and growling. It is an ear-splitting concert, performed as soon as any new arrival is perceived, with the pertinacity of despair, for it is sheer despair that is

depicted on most of the canine faces; despair at the discomforts of confinement, the unaccustomed surroundings, the impending doom.

I shall not forget for a long time to come the look on the face of an aristocratic collie; he looked at me with human eyes, whimpering and whining and unfolding his troubles to me in exquisite dog language, moving body and tail in every possible posture of entreaty and abject submission, and, when I moved away, he pressed his nose and paws against the railings and emitted a cry such as might burst from the shipwrecked on a barren island, who sees the sail on which he built his hopes of deliverance disappear on the horizon. Nevertheless, as soon as the dog has got reconciled to his new surroundings and kennel mates, his condition is by no means the worst. He is fed on scientific principles; he receives hounds' meal (a mixture of meat and meal), and duly soaked in water the well known 'Spratt's Meat Biscuits', which are prepared as a tempting morsel for the canine palate. He obtains exercise in the playground, a railed-in enclosure behind the kennel, where he may run and romp to his heart's content; a shed-roof protects him from the rain, and he can take his rest on a couch lined in the winter with straw. Hence happy is the dog who has not been too fastidiously educated and is not possessed of too delicate nerves; he will settle down very quickly to these states of affairs. When a dog is claimed, the meeting between master and dog is a most touching scene. As soon as the animal hears the sound of his master's voice, he jumps about as if demented, then circles around him with mad leaps, his eyes sparkle with joy, and, when he has been redeemed, he rushes out without even casting a farewell look upon his less fortunate fellow prisoners.

The Annual General Meeting of 1896 saw a return by Sir George to sentimental verse with the sad story of poor Tray:

> *There was grieving in the woodshed,*
> *In the kitchen there were tears,*
> *When the morning showed that Tray was dead,*
> *The friend of many years.*

Ah! I can well remember
How the little children cried,
And lifted up their voices
When the old dog died.

They clasped his rough and shaggy neck,
They called his name in vain,
No more when Tommy whistled
Would Tray bound forth again,
The children ate no breakfast,
But, seated by his side,
They mourn'd their dearest playmate,
When the old dog died.

For thirteen summers he had brought,
The milch cows home at night,
And all that time he'd watched the house
From dark till morning light.
He'd even rock the cradle with a sort of canine pride.
No wonder that the baby wept,
When the old dog died.

He'd go half-way to school with them,
Then stand in lonesome plight,
And slowly wag his bushy tail
Till they were out of sight.
Then trot him home to sleep and snooze
Within his kennel wide—
But Tommy brought the cattle home,
When the old dog died.

There must then surely have been a pause in the proceedings while the audience furtively produced their handkerchiefs and wiped their eyes!

It was at that 1896 meeting that a revolutionary idea was first mooted, then published in the Annual Report that followed, that a suburban branch of the Home should be established.

... Your Committee have had under serious consideration for some time past a much needed proposal for extending the usefulness of the Home by establishing a suburban Branch, whither the better class of dogs could be sent so that an effectual effort may be made to improve their condition, restore them to health, and save a large number of them from the Lethal Chamber . . .

The report went on to say that after a subcommittee that had been set up specially for the purpose had looked at several pieces of land, it had been decided that a plot of $8\frac{1}{2}$ acres at Hackbridge in Surrey had been selected as the most suitable one they had seen for a suburban extension of the Home. On the London, Brighton and South Coast Railway line, this plot was not only adjacent to the station, but only twenty-seven minutes by train from London Bridge, and roughly eight miles from the Home by road. Thanks to a generous donation given by Mrs Grove-Grady, which had been received the year before, it had been possible to pay for the freehold of this meadow for £3,294. Such sums represented really big money in those days, and Mrs Grove-Grady must have been a rich and extremely generous person. Land near the Home in Battersea was ruled out as at that time it was fetching about £7,500 an acre, an amount which seems almost laughable to us in these days when an acre of building-land in central London fetches anything up to £500,000.

The Committee expressed themselves sure that the opening of such an annexe would prove a fitting celebration of the Diamond Jubilee of Queen Victoria, and, while fully aware that there would have to be a considerable outlay of money in the first instance, they were sure that considerable financial benefit would accrue to the Home, as they intended reverting to the practice that had proved so unsuccessful in the early days at Holloway of taking in dog-boarders. An appeal for funds was launched, which resulted in the almost immediate and anonymous donation of £1,000.

The necessary funds were evidently quickly forthcoming, for not only was the land paid for but a reception house was built; it was described as 'spacious, light and sanitary and possessing every facility for receiving and examining the dogs as they enter the Home'.

In reporting the purchase of the site, Sir George, in whose breast sentiment played such a large part, referred to a cemetery devoted to memorials to faithful pets in Hyde Park off the

Bayswater Road, saying that it was full to overflowing. There was, he reported, a corner at Hackbridge that could be devoted to a similar purpose, and he hoped that they would be able to place it at the service of the public. Sir George probably also had in mind the clearly expressed opinion of his Monarch.[14]

This annexe at Hackbridge was opened at the end of October in 1898 by the Duchess of Portland. An extract from the Annual Report gives a picture of this new Home at Hackbridge that is almost beyond belief in these days of motorways and arterial roads:

> The Committee greatly desire to enlist the sympathies of members of the Society on behalf of the new Country Home at Hackbridge, and beg them that they will endeavour to visit the place, and do all they can to induce their friends to journey down and interest themselves in the undertaking. An inspection of the kennels and exercising grounds will reveal the greatly improved conditions under which the dogs are kept, their manifestly better appearance, and the marked signs of happiness they display. The natural beauties of the surrounding, too, are very attractive and cannot fail to be appreciated.
>
> The Home is quite easy to reach by the London, Brighton & South Coast Railway, either from London Bridge or Victoria, and is directly opposite to Hackbridge Station. The return journey can be accomplished either from Hackbridge, or Mitcham Junction (where there is a better train service), a very pleasant walk of exactly one mile from the Home.
>
> For cyclists the run from town is a most agreeable one of about nine miles over excellent roads the whole distance. From the West End the best route is through Clapham, Balham, Tooting and Mitcham, passing over Mitcham Junction railway bridge. Arrangements will be made for taking care of cycles, and for afternoon tea.

The very idea of an 'agreeable' cycle ride nowadays taking the route suggested makes the mind boggle, the sylvan beauties of the Surrey countryside having been swallowed up long since by the engulfing spread of houses and ever-hungry motor traffic.

We cannot finish the story of the nineteenth century without quoting dear Sir George's parting poem, which he delivered from the Chair in 1899. This was to be his last Annual General Meeting, as he was taken ill early the next year, dying a few months later:

Only a dirty black and white dog;
You can see him any day,
Trotting meekly from street to street;
He almost seems to say,
As he looks in your face with wistful eyes:
'I don't mean to be in your way.'
Sometimes he sees a friendly face,
A face that he seems to know,
And thinks that it may be his master
That he lost so long ago,
And even dares to follow him home,
For he loved his master so.
Poor Jack! He's only mistaken again
And stoned and driven back;
But he's used to disappointments now,
And takes up his beaten track—
Nobody's dog, for whom nobody cares,
Poor unfortunate Jack.

But see, there's coming down the street
An honest-featured lad;
He takes this little dog in his arms,
Who looks so forlorn and sad,
With his muddy feet and draggled tail,
And nothing to make him glad;
And wraps in his coat the shivering waif,
And holds in his warm palms
The pitiful paws that, so tired and cold,
Oft scratched in vain for alms;
And Jack peeped forth with a gladdened face
While the world seemed changed to a better place.
A supper of meat, and a nice warm nest,
And his seedy coat brushed clean,
And whether 'tis Jack or Ned sleeps best,

84

I'm sure will never be seen;
And Jack wakes up with a bark of joy,
While Ned is a 'Band of Mercy' boy.

(*Cheers.*)

7 The Twentieth Century

It was not only Sir George Measom's death that heralded in the new century, but also, not very long afterwards, that of Queen Victoria.

In the early years of this century, the problem foremost in the minds of those connected with the Home was that of dog-stealing. By now they were on excellent terms with the police—in fact the chair at the Annual General Meeting of 1903 was taken by Mr Edward Henry, Chief Commissioner of the Metropolitan Police—and at that meeting John Colam of the RSPCA, an old man by now, said: 'It is quite true, moreover, that unless we, acting for this Society, had had the support of the police which they have always freely given, the Home would have gone to pieces . . . it was our alliance with the police more than anything else which enabled the Home to maintain and increase its usefulness . . .'

The following notice was published in *The Times* on 27 February 1903:

NOTICE RESPECTING STOLEN DOGS: Persons who have lost dogs should go to the temporary HOME FOR LOST AND STARVING DOGS, Battersea Park Road, Battersea, where upwards of thirty dogs supposed to have been stolen are being held in safe keeping in separate compartments, and may be inspected pending proceedings at Marlborough Street Police Court for dog-stealing and dog starving.

The outcome of that hearing at Marlborough Street was that William Lee, known as the 'Chinaman', and Conrad Jaeger, a German boot-maker, were convicted and sentenced to hard labour.

There is no doubt at all that this illegal traffic in stolen dogs

The arches under the
railway have always been
utilised

All but one eagerly hoping
that their master has arrived

The spacious first stage of the rebuilding, showing the new offices incorporating the Secretary's flat

Lost, stolen or strayed?

stemmed from the fact that it was all too easy for unscrupulous people to take the animals along to hospitals and sell them for the purposes of vivisection. The Dogs' Home had to make it absolutely clear that they themselves were on the side of the law, and would have nothing whatsoever to do with this illegal traffic.

1906 brought with it a new Dogs' Act, the main provisions of which still stand. Since 1928 anyone finding a dog may, if he wishes to keep it, inform the police and, having fulfilled an obligation to maintain it for a month, may then consider it his property. A report was made by a Working Party on Dogs set up in 1976 under the chairmanship of Lord Houghton, but has not yet been implemented. The Dogs Act 1906 empowered a police officer to seize any dog he truly believed to be a stray. When a dog was wearing a collar bearing an address, then the person whose address appeared on the collar had to be served with a notice in writing stating that the dog had been seized, and was therefore liable to be sold or destroyed if not claimed within seven days. It was made absolutely clear that, if at the end of those seven days the dog had not been claimed by its rightful owner and all expenses incurred by reason of its detention paid for, then the chief officer of police, *or any person authorised by him on that behalf*—i.e., the Dogs' Home at Battersea and other similar institutions which operated in other parts of the country under individually arranged police contracts—would be completely at liberty to cause the dog to be sold or destroyed. A clause was also added saying that no dog so seized should be given or sold for the purposes of vivisection.

The report of the 1976 Working Party advocates that the police might be relieved of their statutory responsibility for dealing with dogs, and that this should then be handed over to local authorities. There were, of course, disastrous consequences when this was attempted at the end of the last century.

The position regarding the legal title to a dog has been made crystal-clear by both magistrates and judges in several cases; they have stated categorically that, after the seven statutory days now required by law for the dog to remain in custody, the dog is the absolute property of the Home in its capacity as agent for the police, and they may dispose of it as they see fit.

However, should a person arrive after those seven days who is clearly the original owner of a dog and the dog has already gone to a new home, the Secretary-General of the Dogs' Home uses his own discretion. The policy generally followed is that of communicating with the new owner and acquainting them with the facts, and then leaving them to make the decision either to keep their new pet or to allow it to return to its original home.

1906 brought great changes to the Dogs' Home, as it had received a complete face-lift, the kennels being rebuilt to the design of Clough Williams-Ellis, probably best known for his unusual complete village in Wales, Portmeirion. Financially the Home was evidently on the up and up at last.

The arrangements that had been made with the police required dogs to be collected from seventy-eight police stations in the County of London, and a further forty-nine in outer London, so in 1909, to ease the burden of this work, two motor and six horse vans were hired from a firm called Tillings. Painted bright red, the vans bore the name of the Dogs' Home in large bold letters on each side, and provided ever-moving advertisements for the Home that were to become a familiar sight in the London streets.

In that same year, Henry Ward, who had been Secretary to the Home since 1893, retired, and was given 'a handsome testimonial', a tray of Sheffield plate on which stood a complete tea and coffee service, subscribed for by the past and present members of the Committee. It was presented to him by the then President of the Home, the Duke of Portland, who had succeeded Lord Onslow in 1889 when Lord Onslow became Governor of New Zealand.

A week or so later what was probably a much more enjoyable party took place. The combined staff of the Battersea and Hackbridge Homes gave a supper and concert in a Hackbridge public house entirely at their own expense, with Mr Ward as the guest of honour. He received another presentation—a framed and autographed photograph of the staff and a 'smoker's companion', which it was hoped would stand in his study. With no ladies present to inhibit the proceedings, the evening took a very merry turn, ending with the linking of arms and the singing of *Auld Lang Syne*. Henry Ward must indeed have been a popular man with his staff.

His place was taken by Mr Guy Guillum Scott, a Barrister-at-Law of the Inner Temple, who had served as an active member of the Committee since 1903, retiring from it only in order to become a candidate for the Secretaryship. This appointment provided another example of family connections playing an important part in the running of the Home, for Guy Guillum Scott's father, Sir Guillum Scott, had been Chairman since the death of Sir George Measom. He himself died just as his son became Secretary, and was succeeded by Mr Percy Thornton, who had been Member of Parliament for the Clapham Division of Battersea.

1911 marked the start of a new Georgian era, and a return to a Monarchy that was not only loved but also revered by the general public. By then, more than a million dogs had passed through the Home, although the figures for that particular year showed a substantial drop. This was put down largely to the fact that during the first half of the year the police were so taken up with preparations for the Coronation of King George V and with strikes and other forms of unrest in the field of labour that the collection of stray dogs had to accept low priority.

After the Great War, people were to look back longingly to the years before it, thinking of them as halcyon times of peace and plenty. But their memories were bound to have been blurred by the horror of the experiences they had shared from 1914 to 1918, when there was hardly a family in Great Britain that did not lose at least one member, whether on land, sea or in the air—and so there were many flaws in their nostalgic dreams. The pre-war British economy was not nearly as healthy as people 'remembered' in later years, and big strikes were common occurrences. The Dogs' Home had been far-seeing, for they introduced an insurance scheme of their own for their employees in 1907. It was not until 1911 that a National Insurance Act making insurance compulsory for workers was introduced, and then only in seven industries at the outset.

The scare of the 'laboratories'—i.e., vivisection—which caused the Dogs' Home so much trouble was largely engendered by the fact that scientific studies in this country, following in the wake of Germany, were increasingly introduced into universities, and serious scientific research was being carried on in most of them. Education in science still did not rank as high, though, in the social and intellectual scale as did education in the subjects of mathematics, theology and the classics.

Active local authorities were providing cleaner, well lit streets, with better water supplies and sanitation, with recreation grounds, free libraries and schools. Democracy was being seen to work, and the result was amusingly described by Sidney Webb whose name appeared in the Home's subscription list:

The individualist town councillor will walk the municipal pavement, lit by municipal gas and cleansed by municipal brooms with municipal water and—seeing by the municipal clock in the municipal market, that he is too early to meet his children coming from the municipal school, hard by the county lunatic asylum and the municipal hospital, will use the national telegraph system to tell them not to walk through the municipal park, but to come by the municipal tramway to meet him in the municipal reading-room, by the municipal museum, art-gallery and library where he intends . . . to prepare his next speech in the municipal town hall in favour of the nationalisation of canals and the increase of Government control over the railway system. 'Socialism, Sir,' he will say, 'don't waste the time of a practical man by your fantastic absurdities. Self-help, Sir, individual self-help, that's what had made our city what it is.'

Battersea Council was not lagging with its reforms. They had new Municipal Buildings; the Electricity Generating Station had been built by the Works Department of the Battersea Borough Council; a children's room had been inaugurated at the Central Library; and the Nine Elms Baths were opened. An Infant's Milk Depot was started by the Borough Council just down the road from the Dogs' Home, and the first Council Housing Estate had been opened in 1903, with the rent of a five-roomed house fixed at eleven shillings and sixpence a week. A Recreation Ground was opened in 1906, and electric tramways traversed the Borough by 1908. The St James' Hospital was opened in 1910, and in that same year a new Library was inaugurated by the Archbishop of Canterbury at the Battersea Polytechnic. The Borough was therefore well abreast of the times.

An attack on the Dogs' Home by *John Bull* in 1911 was not provided with a sitting target this time, as had the attacks made by the press in the early days of the Home. Actions at law, against both John Bull Ltd. and Messrs Odhams Ltd., who were the printers and publishers of the paper, were instantly put in train. It is evident that the Committee were starting to become more worldly. The affair was settled out of Court, an apology was published and adequate costs were arranged. The reason for this change of attitude in the Committee may have been because gradually the substantial part of it was becoming composed of men; the women who had often tended to mix sentiment with business—with, of course, notable exceptions, such as Mrs Tealby and Miss Lloyd (who had come to the rescue of the Home with a very low-interest loan long before)—were gradually dropping out, and their places were being taken by businessmen, barristers and bankers.

In 1912 the number of visitors who came to the Home and the enquiries received there through the post were quite abnormal, and therefore taxed the efforts of the staff, both in the office and in the yard. Letters enquiring about dogs that had been lost were being received from all over the country, and in one case a dog was restored to its owner that had been stolen from as far afield as Manchester.

It was thought that the time was now ripe for yet another extension to the field of work of the institution, and a Home in the north of London was mooted. The Committee was not unanimous about this suggestion, however, for some of them felt that the extra expense that would be incurred would not be justifiable, and some of them were able to call to mind what had happened when the Home was situated in a residential district forty-five years before.

The Cats' Home, which had been very close to being done away with altogether because of a severe outbreak of sickness among its inmates, was happily taking on a new lease of life. Whittington Lodge, its original home, had become too small for the large numbers of cats that were being brought in, so that was converted into an infirmary and quarters for toy dogs, and a new home for the cats was built.

An Out-patients' Clinic was opened at the beginning of October 1912 to provide those people who genuinely could not afford the charges of a qualified Veterinary Surgeon. Mr Guy Guillum Scott, the new Secretary, believed that Battersea's daily haul of strays often reflected a terrible struggle in a poor home: at last, after a great deal of heart-searching, a decision would have to be made, and then the dog would be dumped. After the dog had gone, very likely grandfather would be next, being sent off to the Poorhouse!

The better bred dogs were sent to Hackbridge and they mostly found homes, but for the poor little mongrel, 'well, there was always Nirvana'. This Clinic was a practical attempt to help the poor to keep their pets. A scheme was initiated whereby every life-member of the Society was entitled annually to receive five out-patients' letters, which they were at liberty to distribute to cases brought to their notice of real distress. The people given these letters, on presenting them at the Home, were then issued with cards and their pets became registered patients of the Clinic. With a small charge of sixpence for medicine, the Dogs' Home had instituted their own 'health scheme'. Each clinic afternoon, twice weekly, on Tuesdays and Thursdays, a large number of 'patients' turned up, some carried and some even being brought in a baby's perambulator. The largest number of cases proved to be those caused by inadequate or incorrect feeding—small wonder in those days, when often a whole family would go hungry for want of the wherewithal to buy nourishing food.

During those years the whole of Europe was lying under the shadow of war. Clearly the causes of the war lay far deeper than the mere assasination of an Austrian archduke and his wife at Sarajevo in June 1914, the spark igniting the flame that triggered off the mounting tension. The focal point had always been in the Balkans, and this double murder gave the Austrians a viable excuse for striking down Serbia. She would never have taken this course, with the clear knowledge that the full fury of Russia would descend on her, had she not also been certain that she would receive the complete support of Germany. All possibility of an Anglo-German alliance had been lost by the folly of Kaiser William II of Germany in trusting Kruger, and, more particularly, by his stubborn insistence on building a large navy which served to create a barrier of active mistrust and downright hostility.

The reason for the Kaiser's misguided attempts to form an alliance with Kruger in the 1890s was that Germany, although leading the world in the fields of commerce and of military power, felt she had missed out in the acquisition of territory, especially as she viewed the ever-expanding British. As Sir George Measom had said at the time of Queen Victoria's Golden Jubilee, it was estimated that she ruled over one-fifth of the world's surface—a fact that greatly pleased her, as we learn from letters written at the end of the century by one of her maids of honour, Marie Mallet (née Adeane). Young men who lacked opportunity in these islands were free to go out and seek their fortunes in Australia, Canada, New Zealand and Africa; while Germany could offer nothing in the least comparable for her many pushing young men. Their opportunity, alas, was to be given the chance to fight and fall for the Fatherland in the stinking mud of the trenches a few years later, where about two million young Germans died.

By the time the 1914–18 war broke out, a new block of boarding kennels had been completed at Hackbridge, and were ready just in time to house nearly a hundred working sledge dogs that Ernest Shackleton had sent from Canada, which he intended taking with him on his second Antarctic Expedition. They were all half-breeds, being husky-collie, husky-St Bernard or husky-wolf crosses. Although aloof and with a reputation for savagery, when huskies are domesticated they make excellent companions, growing to love their masters in the same way as other dogs. These huskies of Shackleton's were no exception, for one of the party, Walter How, who died only a few years ago, spoke of the dogs with affection, even remembering some of them individually by name fifty years later.

This enormous, and soon to be famous, pack of dogs was kennelled at Hackbridge for two months completely free of charge, drawing large crowds of sightseers. The field of Antarctic exploration was one that caught the imagination of the general public. One of the Dogs' Home keepers, George Wyndoe, became so expert at handling those large and moderately untamed dogs that he was lent to the expedition to escort the greater number of dogs on the first leg of their journey as far as Buenos Aires.

George Wyndoe had had a chequered career. Before he joined the staff at Hackbridge he had travelled from fairground to fairground, all over Britain, selling patent medicines. On some occasions he had been obliged to beat a hasty retreat, when after a particularly successful day's sales he had taken to replenishing his supplies with ordinary tap water. He had 'the gift of the gab', and remained in the employ of the Home until his retirement; and even then he came back regularly to collect his pension and regale his old friends with tall stories.

On his return from Buenos Aires, however, it was to join up in the Army. During the first months of the war the Battersea staff was decimated, ten men, representing more than a third of the entire man-power, having left to go into the armed services. They went, however, on the definite understanding that they would be reinstated in their former jobs as soon as the war was over—nobody in their innocence expecting it to last more than a few months at the outside—and provision was made by the Home for wives and dependents of the men.

Immediately after the outbreak of war, the number of dogs coming into Battersea fell off for a short time, and this was thought to be because dogs were valued as companions and guards for those left behind, as so many young men had left their families. However, many dogs were brought in to be destroyed, their masters having made desperate but fruitless attempts to find temporary homes for them. There were some bitterly heart-rending scenes in the yard, as those young men, many of whom were destined to be killed themselves, made their last farewells to their bewildered pets.

The clinic that had been running with great success now for several years had to be closed when John Stow Young, the veterinary surgeon in charge, joined up. Luckily, however, it was not long before someone was found to take his place for the duration, and it was re-opened.

John Stow Young joined the Royal Veterinary Corps, and right at the very end of the war, in 1918, he won a Military Cross for conspicuous bravery and devotion to duty near a little place called Guy. While in charge of an Army Veterinary Corps party he came across a large number of wounded horses, which had stampeded, terrified out of their wits by the heavy shell fire. With supreme coolness and courage, and with the help of his men, he managed to catch and calm the frightened animals, eventually restoring order. Then, placing the wounded men he found lying around on the backs of the now quietened horses, he led the whole party back to safety in the face of an enemy advance, bringing also arms and equipment that would otherwise have been abandoned and fallen into enemy hands.

All through the war, conditions at Battersea and Hackbridge

were chaotic. The quarantine kennels were in serious danger of being closed altogether, as they were subjected to an overwhelming influx of dogs picked up by the troops in the trenches, villages and deserted farmhouses of France and Belgium. It is easy to understand how a lonely soldier came to befriend a pathetic starving dog that had been deserted by its fleeing owners. After taking it back with him to endure the rigours of trench-life, when eventually a transport was found to take him home what more natural than that he should take his newfound friend? Alas, distemper swept Hackbridge at this time, and most of the refugee dogs succumbed to it and died.

Nobody realised in the early days of the war that it was going to last for four years, nor that the cream of young manhood was going to be skimmed off the population during those years. The Dogs' Home reflected the position of the whole country, which was split into two factions—those who went and those who stayed. Strangely enough, there is evidence of a certain kind of complacency creeping into the wartime reports of the Committee, in spite of the fact that seven of its members joined up and two of the ones who were too old for active service volunteered for the Anti-Aircraft Corps.

The day-to-day life of the Home went on, with what seemed to be insuperable problems arising daily over food—or, rather, the lack of it. Collection of dogs from the police stations presented great difficulties owing to the acute shortage of petrol in the country as a whole. The one ray of light was that, although expenses went up at an alarming rate, donations and legacies also increased apace, investments growing from the 1910 level of £22,500 to over £50,000 at the end of the war.

By 1916, out of a staff of thirty-six, twenty had gone to war. Their places were filled as far as possible by discharge men from the forces and by men of over military age, but the very fact of their age and disabilities presented even more problems, as the work around the Home has always been physically demanding—many aspects of it needing to be carried out by the young and fit.

However, when the Home Office made a suggestion that, in those days of emergency, the time for the dogs to be kept should revert to three days once more, and that they should then be summarily destroyed, the Committee rose as a man. They made an emphatic statement to the effect that while, as loyal members of the British public, they would of course obey a direct order, it would be regarded as an order of extreme repugnance to the Home as a whole, and would serve to destroy all that had been done by them over the years to improve the lot of the dog. Such an order would, in fact, defeat the object for which the Home had originally been founded, and overcome the principles for which it had fought for more than fifty years.

Happy to relate, nothing more was heard from the Home Office, and everyone at Battersea struggled on until November 1918, when the Armistice was signed.

8 Dogs at War

Towards the end of 1916 on the south coast of England, within sight of the coast of France, there was a large open space dotted about with what appeared to be miniature sentry-boxes, the whole area being surrounded by high hedges and barbed-wire fences. This was the world-famous War Dog School, run under the auspices of the War Office by Colonel Edward Richardson, whose recruits were drawn largely from the Dogs' Home at Battersea.

For years before the outbreak of the 1914–18 war, Richardson had bombarded the military authorities with appeals to be allowed to train dogs for use in battle, but all his pleas had fallen on stony ground, and it was not until the war was well under way that he was at last able to put his ideas into action.

The intelligence and fidelity of the dog has long been recognised as a most valuable asset in the protection of persons and property. In fact, as we saw when we examined the history of the relationship between man and dog, it was the very possession of these qualities that first caused the domestication of the dog. Military commanders have appreciated their worth during many hundreds of years, and dogs have been used with armies all over the world.

The Romans, as well as using them as watchdogs and attacking dogs, forced the unfortunate creatures to swallow metal tubes containing messages; they had been trained to carry these wherever necessary. When they reached their destinations, often after showing great gallantry, they were immediately put to death, hacked open and the metal tubes extracted to divulge the secrets they contained.

Towards the end of the nineteenth century, several continental countries began to explore the possibility of using dogs in warfare, and Germany, Holland, France, Russia and

99

Sweden all started their own schemes, the Germans possessing about 1,500 highly trained dogs by 1914. Germany was also to the fore when it came to the consideration of dogs for police work, for in fact the qualities required for police dogs differ very little from those needed for dogs in war. The same breeds are used, the same discipline, much the same psychology, and very nearly the same training methods. It is really only the greater risk of wounding or of death in the performance of their duties that differentiates military dogs from those used against criminals.

This country was not so quick off the mark, and poor Edward Richardson must have felt that his was a voice crying in the wilderness. It incensed him to see pictures in German papers of English-bred airedales, sheepdogs and collies, bought up in this country by agents sent over from Germany specially for the purpose, being used for military training, and eventually destined to be used in the field against us.

The French had a number of dogs stationed with several of their infantry regiments, and they also gave official encouragement to dog clubs that trained dogs up to high professional standards. However, they did not open an official military dog-training school until about the same time that we did.

The messenger dog was the one that came to the forefront, and had come to stay. Like the tank, it could be said to have been the product of the Great War, for the great success of the dog forces was brought about by the particular conditions that prevailed in that war.

As with all innovations, there were many sceptics at first. But as the casualties among military runners reached alarming proportions, the army at last began to think along Richardson's lines, and considered seriously whether or not dogs could feasibly be expected to take their place. Two questions had to be asked: would the dogs stand up to gunfire, and would they be entirely dependable in all the unexpected conditions of warfare? The dogs themselves provided the answer to these questions: yes. They passed rapidly through the danger areas, often traversing with swift ease land that could not possibly have afforded enough cover for a man—who, in any case, could never have attained the speed essential for safety. A dog could cover difficult terrain in minutes, whereas a man would have taken hours, the dog moreover providing a much smaller and more swiftly moving target. Not only were the lives of runners saved by Richardson's army of strays, but countless others, too, entire units being spared when urgent messages reached their destinations in the shortest possible time, all other means having failed.

For many years Edward Richardson had made a study of what he considered could be the dog's part in what was then called modern warfare. He had built up a large kennel of dogs with which he and his wife made constant experiments. Rather naturally, he did not confine his attentions only to army uses, but also covered police work. Many provincial police forces used his dogs successfully for patrolling suburban areas and therefore agreed with his principles. It was only the army that stubbornly refused to listen and could not be persuaded to experiment. People from all over the world consulted Edward Richardson, asking his advice on how to obtain safety for themselves and their property by the controlled use of trained dogs. Owners of tea and coffee estates, sugar plantations, poultry and animal farms, prisons, rubber estates, large rambling mansions, factories and docks were all suffering from the difficulty of recruiting men of a suitable calibre who could be relied upon to carry out effective guard duties; and it was these people who came to Richardson, who treated each case individually, as he believed that they all presented different problems.

Airedales, collies, sheepdogs, whippets, retrievers and deerhounds were used either as messengers or as sentries, while Great Danes, boarhounds and mastiffs were in demand as watchdogs. The duty of this second category was not to tackle an intruder but to give the alarm, so watchdogs needed comparatively little training. It is interesting to find that the airedale, which is not often seen nowadays, in particular was found to be able to adapt itself in an amazing way to changes in climate, from near arctic to tropical, and was also found to be an all-round courageous, reliable, hardy and intelligent animal. In those days the breed abounded and there were plenty of them to be found, especially in the Dogs' Home at Battersea.

Before the war, Richardson had paid a fascinating visit to Russia, where the Tsar himself took a personal interest in the training of dogs. While there, he acted as a judge at some army trials of military dogs, his co-judges being two German officers.

Although Richardson felt himself bound to admire the efficient organisation of the German kennels, he was sure that we could find and train more suitable dogs for the job. He felt that the Germans put too much emphasis on the actual mechanical obedience training, and did not pay enough attention to canine psychology, neglecting the use of the dog's undoubted quick intelligence and ability to think for itself and act sensibly on the spur of the moment. The German methods were painstaking and extremely slow, and Richardson could see clearly that vast numbers of trained dogs were going to be needed in a hurry, for he envisaged them guarding bridgeheads, magazine factories and other valuable property of military importance.

As soon as the war broke out, he immediately offered his whole kennel of trained dogs to the War Office, but his generous offer was turned down out of hand.

Dispirited by this rejection, he turned his attention to the training of dogs to trace the wounded in the battlefield. The British, in their innocence, were convinced of the inviolability of the Red Cross, but were to find their illusions quickly shattered. When the French army hurriedly sent some of their ambulance dogs with their keepers to the front line in the early feverish days of the war, both men and dogs were brutally shot down in cold blood. The bitter fact was that the only ambulance units that were used with any degree of success were those of the German army itself, when the Russians were in retreat on the eastern front.

Richardson offered his services to the British Red Cross Society, and actually found himself sent to Belgium together with a group of trained ambulance dogs. Making his way to Brussels in front of the British army, it was only to find the Belgians in full retreat as the enemy entered the city from the other side. He managed to get back to Ostend with his dogs, but found conditions there impossible; in fact, after a few abortive weeks, the French War Office entirely forbade the use of dogs with their army.

However, during 1914 and 1915, Richardson received a number of individual requests from officers serving at the front for dogs to use for sentry and patrol work. He did his best to supply these, also sending some to the Belgians. At the same time, possibly motivated by advice from Richardson, many letters of request for dogs were being addressed to the War Office by senior serving officers.

During the winter of 1915, Richardson received a request from a colonel in the Royal Artillery for dogs to keep up communications between an outpost and the main battery during heavy bombardment, when field telephones were found to be useless and the risk to runners too great to be considered. Richardson quickly and painstakingly experimented with the dogs he already had on hand, and finally he was satisfied that there were two that would be capable of carrying messages safely back to base for anything up to two miles. These two dogs were airedales recruited from the Dogs' Home, Battersea, and they left for France on 31 December, and they went straight to Thiepval under the escort of a gunner. It is evident that they must have been very intelligently handled when they arrived, for, although they had received their initial training far from the battlefield, they settled down immediately and were to carry regular messages. After one successful sortie, Colonel Winter reported:

> . . . After being led up through communication trenches during darkness, they went forward as soon as the attack was launched, passing through the smoke barrage . . . Both dogs reached Brigade headquarters, travelling a distance as the crow flies of 4,000 yards over ground they had never seen before and over an exceptionally difficult terrain. . .

These two courageous dogs, which up to a few weeks before had been strays in the streets of London, were destined to pave the way to the recognition of Richardson's dreams. At long last the authorities made formal enquiries into the possibility of setting up some sort of training establishment for the provision of messenger dogs for the army. Richardson's moment of triumph had come, and he must have been elated when he presented himself at the War Office, whence he had been called to discuss the matter in full. He was only too happy to make concrete suggestions, which were acted upon immediately. The school at Shoeburyness was founded, that area being chosen because it was within earshot of constant gunfire, and therefore was thought ideal for the work.

The course of instruction given to the messenger dogs who

were to carry despatches close to and within the firing line was both elaborate and, by necessity, comparatively prolonged— although not as long as the course given by the Germans. The job for which they were trained puts one in mind of the work of a homing pigeon, where each bird has to return home to its loft when released in unfamiliar surroundings. In the same way, the dogs were taught to return to their kennels, where their individual trainers waited with food. It was essential that each should make a beeline for its home, no matter what obstacles lay in its way, carrying messages through lines of firing infantry; negotiating all kinds of barbed-wire entanglements and other difficult obstacles; rushing through clouds of gas—not only performing these amazing feats, but carrying them out with the minimum of delay, by day or night.

The training began with the dog having to return to its kennel from a short distance away. On its arrival it was immediately given a titbit and made much of by its keeper. Gradually, day by day, the distances were increased and more and more obstacles were put in its way, until at last the dog was capable of covering up to four or five miles at break-neck speed in order to deliver its message safely.

The men were expected to handle only three or four dogs, and they came from all walks of life; but, as might be expected, gamekeepers and poachers proved the most suitable people for the job. The essence of the whole thing lay in the personal touch, so when the dog pupil eventually went overseas it was with its known and loved trainer, and it also took its own familiar collapsible kennel on active service. No punishment of any kind was ever meted out, this being a very strict rule that had always been adhered to by Colonel and Mrs Richardson ever since they had embarked on their joint training of dogs. If, as sometimes was the case, a dog proved useless, it was immediately dismissed, and, unhappy to relate, ended up in the lethal chamber at Battersea.

The messages themselves were carried in little leather wallets fastened securely to the inside of the dogs' collars, and the dogs themselves were treated as soldiers, drawing regular rations and having their own 'defaulter sheets' on which was recorded any lapse from discipline, or anything else worthy of note. The only differences were they had only one meal a day and that they drew no pay.

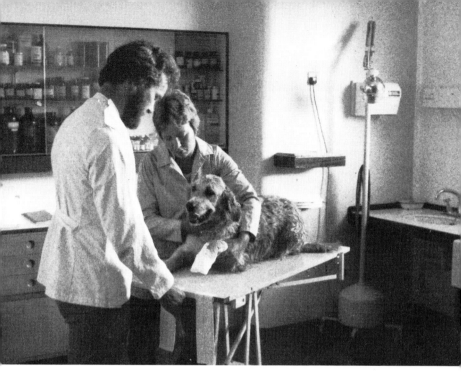

Scenes from *Dog Days*, a documentary film about the Home: (*above*) the retriever with the broken leg is in fact Sugar, much-loved pet of Colonel Sweeney, Director-General of the Home; (*below*) the busker's dog eventually finds himself in the Home

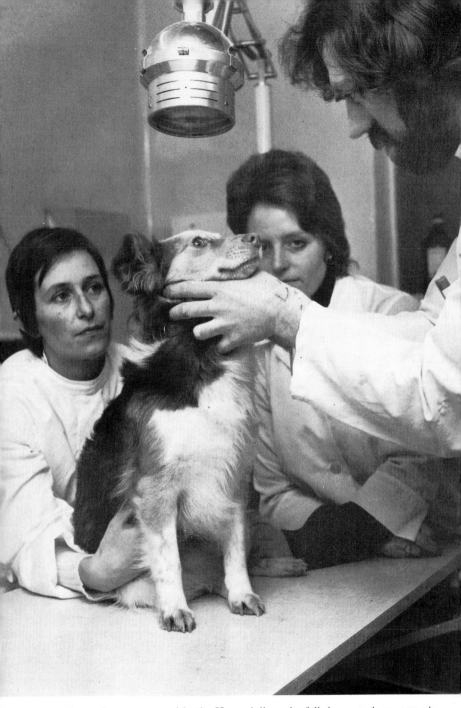

A veterinary surgeon visits the Home daily and a full-time veterinary nurse is employed

It was not to be long before Colonel Richardson received glowing reports of his dogs, and very soon a supervisor from the Royal Engineers received a training at Shoeburyness, being then sent out to organise a complete messenger dog service in France. Up until that point dogs had been sent only to individual battalions whose commanding officers had asked specifically for despatch dogs.

The supervisor soon found that better results were obtained by forming the keepers with their dogs into a complete unit, and a central kennel was set up at Étaples. From there they were posted to sectional kennels behind the front line, each of which comprised about forty-eight dogs and sixteen men in the charge of a sergeant.

Class after class of men and their dogs was sent to France after their five-week training course, and eventually the school was so famous that it became a showpiece, and a flood of requests was received from people who wanted to visit it and watch the work that went on. Indeed, there were so many visitors that a special day had to be set aside each week for them so that the serious training work should not be set back in any way. Sir John French himself was one of the visitors.

The first World War saw 7,000 dogs killed in action, and many times that number died from wounds and poison gas. Alaskan huskies, alsatians, sheepdogs, airedales, terriers, lurchers and a host of shaggy mongrels, nearly all of them from Dogs' Homes, and mostly from Battersea (although some were given as outright gifts to Colonel Richardson by people who wanted to help the war effort, in the full knowledge that there could be no positive guarantee of their eventual return), fought and died, unheralded and, for the most part, unmourned, except by their handlers, who must have developed a great bond of love and friendship with the dogs they trained so well.

Perhaps the most moving story of all, which serves to show to the full the extent of Colonel Richardson's dreams and their fulfilment, is contained in the following newspaper report:

In the British War Museum is a small wooden stand . . . to the memory of Airedale Jack, a hero of the Great War.

Just a dog . . . but a hero who in 1918 saved a whole British battalion from being annihilated by the enemy.

Airedale Jack was sent over to France as a messenger

and guard. There was a big push on, and he was taken by the Sherwood Foresters to an advance post.

The battle raged, and things went badly against the Foresters. The enemy sent across a terrific barrage, cutting off every line of communication with headquarters, four miles behind the lines.

It was certain that the entire battalion would be wiped out unless reinforcements could be secured from headquarters, but how? It was impossible for any man to creep through the walls of death that surrounded them.

But there was just one chance—Airedale Jack. Lieutenant Hunter slipped the vital message into the leather pouch attached to the dog's collar. A pat on the head and then simply: 'Goodbye, Jack . . . Go back, boy.'

The battalion watched Jack slip quietly away, keeping close to the ground and taking advantage of whatever cover there was, as he had been trained to do.

The bombardment continued, and the shells fell all around him. A piece of shrapnel smashed the dog's lower jaw . . . but he carried on. Another missile tore open his tough, black and tan coat from shoulder to haunch—but on he went, slipping from shell-crater to trench.

With his forepaw shattered, Jack had to drag his wounded body along the ground for the last three kilometres. There was the glaze of death in his eyes when he reached headquarters—but he had done a hero's work and saved the battalion.

Jack, a Battersea dog, was presented with a posthumous VC.

9 The Birth of Publicity

The aftermath of the Great War brought with it the birth of publicity and propaganda as we now know it. The war was to bring about a radical change in the hitherto prevalent style of journalism, providing a lighter touch altogether and a less laboured form of humour.

The declaration of the Armistice on 11 November 1918 had been celebrated with exultant enthusiasm by ecstatic crowds drawn from all classes of people. It seemed that at last the long nightmare was over, and surely there must be the dawn of a new and happier age. Soldiers returned to their homes, and all seemed to be well, and for a time the country basked in what was in fact a time of artificial prosperity. Prices were rising all the time, but wages went up correspondingly. At the election held just after the end of the war, Lloyd George, who had promised to create a land fit for heroes, was returned with an overwhelming majority. The nation was grateful to him, thinking of him as the organiser of victory, so this result was his own personal triumph.

However, the promises that he had made so glibly while the war was raging seemed far from easy to achieve. The miners, who had patriotically held their hand during the war years, put in some sharp demands, and there was also a serious railway strike in 1919. There was an acute housing shortage, hardly any having been built during the war years, and unemployment became rife, as many ex-soldiers returned to civilian life only to find that over-age men or even women had taken their place, and found it impossible to gain employment. A slump followed which reached alarming proportions.

All this was, of course, reflected in the receipts of donations to the Home, so it urgently needed every scrap of publicity it could possibly get.

When, in 1918, the *Daily Mirror*, ever-mindful of the value of publicity to the Dogs' Home, carried an appealing picture of a tiny black pekinese, saying that she was the smallest inmate in the Home, and that her days were numbered unless a good home could be found for her, Battersea was inundated with offers of help. Sacks of mail arrived by every post, and altogether over fifteen hundred letters and a hundred and fifty telegrams were received, a special clerk having to be taken on to deal with a constant stream of telephone calls. The happy—and possibly contrived—outcome was that the photograph was recognised by the original owner of the little dog from whom it had been stolen three months earlier. There was a joyful reunion with plenty of attendant publicity, and the Dogs' Home undoubtedly benefited from it all.

Just before the end of the war, Guy Guillum Scott gave up his position as Secretary, returning to the Committee, and his place was taken by Mr Guy Rowley.

At about that time a lady member of the Committee asked whether it would be possible to adopt electrocution as a form of humane slaughter. She had probably heard that this method was in fact becoming generally used, especially in the States, and a machine had been installed at an institution in Islington. The answer to her question was that, when some improvements had been made to the Islington machine, it was hoped to introduce such a machine at Battersea. The matter went into abeyance for a few years, and was not brought up again until 1921. That year the audience at the Annual General Meeting were told that the RSPCA had destroyed the startling number of some 40,000 cats during 1920 by electrocution. They used a machine in which the animal was put into a drawer, and when dead looked for all the world as if it were merely sleeping. The use of this method for dogs had been gone into, but it appeared that their harder, hornier paws and their enormous variations in weight made what, up to then, were insuperable difficulties, as a change of voltage for each animal would be needed.

So the matter went once more into abeyance, not being raised again until 1934, when it appears that the practical electrical problems had been overcome, and an efficient machine was at last installed at Battersea. Modified and improved versions of this electrothanater have been in use ever since, the latest one, installed in 1954, having the full approval of the

British Veterinary Association and being apparently virtually foolproof. It produces an instantaneous and totally pain-free death for the animals on which it is used. Destruction of the dogs and cats is always distressing, but so far no one has been able to come up with a more humane way of carrying out this unpleasant but necessary task, bearing in mind the large numbers that sometimes have to be dealt with. However, recently further modifications were recommended and have been carried out following the report of a special subcommittee set up under Professor Formston of the Royal Veterinary College, who is now on the Committee of the Home, to look into the whole question of euthanasia of animals.

1919 saw another severe outbreak of rabies in Britain, thought to have been caused by the smuggling through a west country port of a single dog by a returning soldier. This one dog was to cause an outbreak responsible for 816 reported cases, though only 319 of these were confirmed, and it took five years before it was finally stamped out. It was essential that stringent measures should be taken, and so another Muzzling Order was introduced, bringing with it all the old attendant problems. This time the powers that be declared that the old type of leather muzzles were useless and insisted that wire cages should be substituted; this caused an immediate and, needless to say, profitable black market in these cages, for a certain section of backstreet traders had learnt all about speedy 'under-the-counter' transactions during the war, and so the muzzles were to be procured only at vastly inflated prices.

At the same time, the Ministry of Agriculture tightened up the quarantine controls, as the country was being literally flooded with dogs brought back by returning troops. There was a therefore correspondingly greater demand for quarantine space, and two hundred temporary kennels had to be erected post-haste at Hackbridge at the Ministry's direct request, plus a further five hundred that were paid for by the RSPCA.

The wages bill of the Home rose alarmingly from £2,724 to £5,301 per annum, this rise reflecting in part the general economic situation but in the main being accounted for by the urgent need to recruit more staff at Hackbridge to deal with the inundation of quarantine boarders. However, this particular crisis brought a bonus in the form of £7,758 in boarding fees, representing an increase of more than £7,500 over the previous year's figures. The quarantine takings were to drop dramatically the following year, as the number of dogs entering the country gradually became fewer and fewer.

It is very distressing to note, however, that out of the 2,236 stray cats that were received in the Home, only 107 were sent to new homes.

The most famous Hackbridge quarantine boarder was a St Bernard called Riffel which had been brought home, perhaps somewhat misguidedly, from a Swiss holiday by the Prime Minister, Lloyd George. A short article in a paper called *The Passing Show* said:

> . . . I like the look of him and am sure that when he is released he will be quite able to fetch the Prime Minister back to Downing Street in case he ever goes astray again.

When Riffel was collected by Lloyd George, still Prime Minister, *The Star* made the following comments:

> Riffel, the Premier's St Bernard dog, left for Chequers today, and the staff at Downing Street is still busy mending the carpets and putting the furniture back where it came from.
>
> He stayed only about twelve hours at No 10 but it was quite enough; and on the advice of a consulting architect it was decided to move him into larger premises at once. Otherwise the Coalition headquarters might have collapsed and brought the Government and the Foreign Office down with it.

The Annual General Meeting at the Dogs' Home that year was in fact disrupted by the fact that Colonel Sir Charles Burn MP, who was to have taken the chair, was unable to leave the House of Commons as the Government had had a defeat the previous day. When Lloyd-George's 1918 Parliament had lasted four years, the Coalition broke down and was followed by a short Conservative Government (1922–23) under Bonar Law and Mr Baldwin. This was broken up by the death of Bonar Law, and then there was a very short-lived but historically important Labour Government under Ramsay MacDonald. The Liberal party shrank and almost disappeared from the field of politics, and then the influence of the Labour party went into a decline. So it was a strong Tory government that was called upon to deal with the General Strike of 1926 when Mr Baldwin had broken off negotiations suddenly, owing to a misunderstanding, and everything suddenly and completely came to a complete halt.

It says a lot for the staff relations under the secretaryship of Guy Rowley that not one man came out on strike, either at Battersea or at Hackbridge—although of course they had never felt the need to be allied to a trade union.

Dogs from Battersea hit the headlines in the 'twenties. Lupino Lane, the famous acrobat and songster, a member of the Lupino family that had been well known as acrobats since 1780, who was to sweep the country with his Lambeth Walk ten years later, chose a nice bull terrier from Battersea. On his way home, he felt worried about the animal, which was panting and seemed generally distressed, so he called in to see a veterinary surgeon. Imagine his amazement, when, an hour later he became the owner not of one bull terrier but of five!

The well-known photographer and big-game hunter of the nineteen-twenties, Cherry Kearton, bought a small fox terrier for 7/6d from the Dogs' Home that was destined to win the coveted prize of a lion's mane when it was on safari in Africa.

Kearton visited the Home to find a small dog to take with him as a companion on an expedition that he was planning. '. . . She had a silly little stump of tail, which began to wag as soon as she saw me. I stood in front of her kennel and laughed: the tail wagged faster than ever.'

What an incredible change it must have been for this little dog that had known only the streets of London to find herself in the wilds of Africa. The purpose of the expedition was to photograph lions in their natural habitat, a most difficult and dangerous occupation in those days long before Land Rovers and game reserves.

Pip was to prove a dauntless and tenacious little animal. One day news was received at the camp that there were two man-eating lions at large near a native village, so Kearton set off armed only with his camera, accompanying eleven young Maasai warriors with spears. Four Somali horsemen rode forward as scouts, to try to entice the lions to come closer. The young Maasai warriors formed themselves into a crescent-shaped line, but, just as they were advancing slowly and cautiously, Pip appeared suddenly at Kearton's side, very excited and eager not to be left out of the fun. A moment later, the party came face to face with the two lions, furiously angry, snarling and tearing at the earth with their forepaws, a terrifying sight. Attack after attack by the spearmen failed, as they could not get near enough to their prey to sink their spears into them. At last the lions bounded off, but the trackers knew that one of them was lying hidden somewhere not far away. Then Kearton had a brainwave. He wondered whether Pip might help, and loosed her hoping that she would use her nose to mark the animal, and by her shrill barks would enable the spearmen to move swiftly, close in and finish it off. Pip, ever eager for action, dashed off and, to everyone's amazement, dived into the dried-up bed of a stream and disappeared. That instant there came a terrible roar from the very place where Pip had vanished, and minutes later it was all over. The lion lay dead, but there also was Pip, still growling and holding the lion's tail firmly clenched between her teeth. She had distracted its attention, giving a warrior the opportunity to creep up and thrust his spear straight through the beast's heart. But, as he did so, Pip had rushed round and sunk her teeth into the tail, utterly refusing to let go.

It is the custom with the Maasai tribe that the man who takes the lion's tail is entitled to its mane—a great triumph and honour. So there was this dauntless little Battersea stray laying claim to the mane of a man-eating lion and earning for herself the nickname of 'Simba', the lion.

In 1923, a little fox-terrier bitch that had been known to be living under one of the buildings in the Judges' Triangle at the Law Courts for nine years, having been fed daily by somebody who worked nearby, was caught at last. She was on her way to the RSPCA for destruction when the Dogs' Home intervened and said it could find her a home, which it did, and she ended her days happily in Hendon. After her capture, two hundredweight of bones were found hidden in her little lair.

1924 saw an unaccountable return to vast numbers of dogs being brought into the Home, the numbers having risen from 13,540 in 1921, to 23,389 in 1923, and then to 32,003, the largest figure since the eighteen-nineties when the duties of the police were taken over by local councils for a few mistaken months. The only explanation that could be found was that the sharply rising prices were causing people to abandon their pets whole-sale.

One dog taken from the Home proved to be so musical that its new owner was no longer able to play what he liked on his piano, but had to turn his skills to Chopin and to nothing else. A Chopin ballade or nocturne made the dog motionless, a silly grin on its face, but a Liszt rhapsody sent him howling out of the room.

The price of a dog licence presented one of the most burning problems of post-war London. 'Dear old thing,' said one pensioner of his ten-year-old dog, finding himself unable to afford the 7/6d licence, 'I have no one to speak to—only him—all the week. I love him.' Happy to relate, in this case the Dogs' Home advanced the money for the licence, as they did with many other cases of proved hardship.

Year after year in early January, the newspapers were full of reports of abandoned dogs when licences became due for renewal. 7/6d seems a paltry amount of money to us in these inflationary days, but fifty or sixty years ago it represented just that little bit over and above the family income that was impossible to raise, especially as licences fell due on 1 January, just after Christmas when expenses are always heavy. People were prepared to go hungry and share their food with their dogs, but very often they were unable to find that pitifully small sum of hard cash.

The Home, surprisingly as it was in the middle of London, was instrumental in returning several foxhounds to their packs in the nineteen-twenties. The Old Berkshire, while hunting near Abingdon, seventy miles from London, found themselves short of a hound at the end of the day. It was eventually picked up at Mitcham only twenty-four hours later and sent to the Dogs' Home. Another bitch hound, lost when the Old Surrey and Burstow were hunting near East Grinstead in Sussex, was found at Wallington in the Dogs' Home area. A prize bitch hound, only just entered to fox-hunting, was lost by the Surrey Union during a run over Earlswood Common and was found in Bromley, Kent, nearly three weeks later. Fortunately foxhounds are always earmarked for easy identification, and it was therefore possible for the Home to return them immediately to their correct packs.

In 1928 the National Dog Week Movement opened a branch

in this country, the mother organisation being a body that called itself by the rather ambitious name of 'The World League for Dog Welfare'. Its aims were to give financial assistance to deserving animal welfare organisations, and also to educate the owners of dogs in their duties and responsibilities towards their pets. The amazing sum of £20,000 was subscribed in less than a year, and this money was used for the re-establishment on what were then described as 'sound and modern' lines of the Canine Department of the Royal Veterinary College, and also for the setting up and endowment of a professorial chair in Canine Medicine and Surgery.

The National Dog Week Movement was helped enormously in its work by another organisation launched in the same year from an office in the City by Captain H. E. Hobbs and known as the Tailwaggers' Club, with branches in Toronto and New York. The Tailwaggers' Club swept the country. 2/6d was all that was required for life-membership, and for this small amount a dog was entitled to its own number engraved on a disc that would enable it to be immediately identified should it be lost, and thus returned home. An excellent newsletter was published each month carrying a wealth of information and useful articles.

It was reported three years later that the foundation of these two organisations had the direct result of the number of dogs in the Home falling from the devastating and all-time record number of 36,000 in 1926 down to a more manageable—although still far too high—25,000 in 1929.

During the 1930s the Tailwaggers' Club continued to have a boom, and it formed an alliance with the *Daily Mirror*, launching a lost-dog service for registered readers of that newspaper, and running highly successful 'dog nights' at London restaurants.

In the meantime, crises were having to be faced at Hackbridge. In 1928 an extension was required to be built when the Ministry of Agriculture extended their quarantine regulations to include cats. Two years later, Guy Rowley, then in his final year as Secretary, had spoken with confidence about the future of the kennels at Hackbridge, saying with truth that they had become a very large concern, and adding that the boarding section was full to bursting as more and more people were beginning to appreciate the need for first-class accommodation of the sort provided there for their pets when they went on holiday. Legacies to Battersea had risen to an astonishing total of £20,455, so things were looking very rosy for the future.

However, the following year was to bring a substantial decrease in the number of boarders at Hackbridge, and the Committee, perhaps in view of the great depression that was beginning to be felt all over the world, began to have second thoughts about the wisdom of running a second establishment at all, having regard to the heavy expenditure it incurred with relatively small returns.

Mr Moss-Blundell, who took the Chair at the Annual General Meeting in 1931, had been a member of the Committee for 24 years, joining it after his retirement as a full-time civil servant at the Board of Agriculture (as it was then called), and he very surprisingly referred to Hackbridge as being something of a 'Swan Song'. He told his audience that the Ministry of Agriculture was reverting to its original policy of licensing quarantine dogs to the private premises of veterinary surgeons.

It is difficult to know from what source Moss-Blundell drew this fact, as only three years after he had retired from the Board of Agriculture the Committee at Battersea had been asked by that Board to set up Hackbridge as a quarantine station; ten years later the Board asked for an extension of the kennels to be made to accommodate the overwhelming numbers of dogs that were being brought back by returning servicemen. It was this addition of quarantine kennels that had led to the paying boarders outnumbering the dogs sent down from Battersea to convalesce, which in fact defeated the purpose for which Hackbridge had been intended: the original concept was, of course, that it would prove an ideal place in which dogs that had suffered hardship in the streets could be nursed back to health, and then eventually found good homes.

The strict quarantine rules had required the daily visit of a veterinary surgeon, in the person of Captain Stow Young, to the premises, but at no time had the Board (later to be known as the Ministry) of Agriculture required Hackbridge to be licensed under a resident veterinary surgeon.

In 1931, the question of the Dogs' Home being incorporated as a registered Charitable Institution was raised. A resolution was moved suggesting that the necessary steps should be taken, this being a very far-seeing move on the part of the Committee. The actual certificate of incorporation was not granted by the Board of Trade until the end of 1933, and then it drew a great deal of criticism from the general public. At first many people were under the impression that the effect of this would be to change the association from a charitable institution to a commercial undertaking, and the Committee had to go to some pains to explain that they were only following the precedent of other old-established animal charities, including the RSPCA; the certificate of incorporation as a registered charity would, in fact, have the effect of raising the status of the Dogs' Home, and would give it the foundation of a sound and stable constitution, removing many of the difficulties with which an unincorporated body had to contend, in view of the birth of bureaucracy that was then taking place.

The following year saw a really ominous note in the Annual Report of the year's proceedings. A Hackbridge subcommittee had been set up during the year, and evidently the expense of maintaining the second Home efficiently had so worried a certain section of the Committee that they felt immediate action should be taken. Offers for the purchase of part or the whole of the premises had been received, and were in process of being carefully considered. They were particularly concerned because the large block of kennels put up by the RSPCA immediately after the war for the purpose of the emergency kenneling of two to three hundred quarantine dogs would shortly have to be replaced or scrapped altogether. The loss of that extra accommodation would result in a radical reduction of the earning capacity of the establishment, whereas the building of new kennels would not be financially viable.

The Chair at the Annual General Meeting was taken by Professor Sir Frederick Hobday, the world-famous veterinary surgeon, who spoke in glowing terms about the work of both homes. He mentioned the excellent work carried out in the clinic, and also spoke more especially about the good work that was being carried out at Hackbridge, saying that it compared more than favourably with any other quarantine kennels he himself had seen anywhere in the world. However, in spite of this, there was obviously a faction on the Committee that felt that the work done at Hackbridge should be left to private enterprise, and the following year they were to have their way.

In July there was trouble over the Police contracts. The Commissioner of the Metropolitan Police gave notice of his intention of terminating the contracts under which the Home received and dealt with stray dogs under the Dogs' Act. New tenders for the service were invited, but it was pointed out that to meet the requirements of the Commissioner it would be necessary to open a new home north of the River Thames, and to erect and equip there a thoroughly modern range of kennels and exercising yards.

The result of this edict was that a branch of the Home was opened at Bow in September, 1935, the year King George V died. It had dealt with three thousand dogs by the end of that year, but was destined never to flourish and thrive. However, its opening necessitated the sale of Hackbridge, which went as a going concern to Spratts, who had made an offer of £10,000 on behalf of one of their subsidiary companies, the Dogs' Sanatorium Ltd, after an offer had been refused by the Committee from a cable company for the site alone. It is ironical to relate that Spratts eventually sold the premises for a quarter of a million pounds in 1970—to a cable company.

Spratts brought with them their own Veterinary Surgeon, Mr R. H. Clarke, which meant that Captain Stow Young, who had done so much for the Home, was made redundant. He was given a grant, although there is no record of how much this was, and eventually he set up practise in Wallington, severing his connection with the Dogs' Home altogether. By a strange quirk of coincidence, the veterinary surgeon employed by Spratts who succeeded Mr Clarke, Mr Frank Beattie, was also made redundant in 1970 when the premises were sold, and he too set up practice in Wallington, and spoke very highly of Stow Young's previous work there.

Battersea dogs continued to hit the headlines, but it is not surprising that the items considered newsworthy were those that were either extravagant or pathetically sad.

A Battersea dog went to live in a comfortable Chelsea home on the day her master was buried in a pauper's grave only a mile or two away. George Clark, an ex-serviceman, had tramped the streets of London for weeks in a vain attempt to find himself a job. All his efforts proved in vain, and, down to his last few shillings, he emptied them all in the gas-meter, turned on the gas-oven and put his head inside. When his body was eventually found, his dog, Florrie, who had escaped death, was found guarding her master; although she was taken to the police station, she managed on two separate occasions to escape and run back to the lonely little bedsittingroom where her master had died.

Gracie Fields, who was just becoming really famous, borrowed some dogs from the Home in 1932 to act with her in a film called *Looking on the Bright Side*. In reporting this, one newspaper made much of the fact that, by the time the film was released, in all probability the dogs appearing in it would be ghosts, as they would have had to be destroyed. Needless to say, the result of this sob-story was an avalanche of offers of homes, Gracie herself keeping a big airedale that had become so fond of her, and she of it, that she could not bear to let it go.

A famous greyhound called Oak Top disappeared from the Catford Stadium kennels, but it was soon discovered. The people who had stolen it had dyed it ginger, but abandoned the animal when the dye started to run, and the secret came out when a streaky greyhound appeared at the Dogs' Home.

In 1935, at the height of the depression, the Tailwaggers' Club, recognising only too well the difficulties experienced by many dog-lovers in finding the money to renew their dog licences as they fell due on New Year's Day, launched an ingenious scheme whereby it was possible to buy twopenny stamps throughout the year that could eventually be exchanged for a dog licence. Cards were provided on which the stamps could be stuck, and these were distributed among vendors of dog foods, branches of the RSPCA, sub-post offices and the many little corner shops that still abounded in those days. On each card were five blank squares, and those who could afford to do so were asked to affix stamps on them as a small contribution towards the expenses incurred by the printing and distribution of the whole scheme. Many people filled in cards on behalf of their less well-off dog-owning friends, and the whole thing led to a feeling of goodwill and kindliness, a good example being that of a dog called Sandy.

Sandy was a Tailwagger, and he and his mistress enrolled nearly 1,300 new members and raised enough money to buy more than a hundred licences for dogs less well off than himself. Later on, the pair of them collected £60 in shillings to provide a guide dog for the blind, then an innovation.

10 The War to End All Wars

At the Dogs' Home, the Munich Crisis did not appear to give rise to much concern, and afforded only the slightest of mentions on the Annual Report for 1938, although it was said that plans had hastily been made for dealing with a state of emergency should it actually arise. Guy Guillum Scott said: 'Happily the storm blew over for the time being, and this has afforded the opportunity for completing arrangements in consultation with the Authorities, should the present state of general unrest lead to the actual outbreak of war.'

The 'actual outbreak of war' the following September called for the immediate putting into action of the emergency plans that had been set up. It was decided that the Finance and General Purposes Committee should act *pro tem* for the full Committee, as it might be impossible to guarantee a quorum for a full Committee meeting each month. This was to be called the War-Time (Executive) Emergency Committee, of which Sir Charles Hardinge took the Chair. Any member of the Committee who happened to be available was entitled to serve on this Emergency Committee, which did in fact continue to meet each month right through the war years.

The Bow Home, which had never been a success, closed down very soon, although a night-watchman had to be maintained in case of fire. It was destined never to be re-opened, and was eventually sold in 1954.

There seem to have been extremely good staff relations under the leadership of Mr Healey Tutt, who had able Superintendents serving under him: Ball at Battersea and Carstairs at Bow—who later moved back to help at Battersea—with Mrs Witherow running the office. The threat of fire was uppermost in Healey Tutt's mind, the Home being in an extraordinarily vulnerable position, standing as it did in a triangle made by two

121

railways and a main road, with the Battersea Power Station a few hundred yards away and two gasometers right behind it. Mr Tutt elected to sleep in the paint-shed to act as a fireguard, and did so for the next five years. He took his duties and his responsibilities very much to heart; eventually, when he wanted to join the local Auxiliary Fire Service as well, he had to be restrained by the Committee and persuaded to confine his fire-watching duties to the Home itself.

Defence measures that came into operation in England included immediate blackout, followed shortly afterwards by the rationing of food. Children were labelled and sent to the country, and compulsory conscription was quickly introduced. The Treasurer of the Home, Captain Daniell, was called up, his place on the Committee being taken by his wife, and three other members went off to join their Units, 'somewhere in England'. Five members of the staff were also called up for active service.

A number of animal first-aid casualty clearing stations were organised by a body set up called the National ARP Animal Committee, on which the Home had a representative. Eight of these were for horses, and dogs and cats were to be dealt with at the Dogs' Home and seven other clinics in various parts of London, although the actual publicity regarding first-aid arrangements for animals was not in fact launched until the summer of 1940; the Blitzkrieg had been raging since April, and the evacuation of our troops from Dunkirk had just taken place. Owners of small animals were warned in the press and over the wireless to keep them indoors after the air-raid sirens had sounded. If dogs or cats received minor injuries the onus would rest on the owners to get them to the nearest clinic; but should they be badly injured then emergency action would need to be taken. The RSPCA started to arrange an evacuation scheme for animals, but this had to be abandoned when the blitz got under way in earnest.

In March 1940 an enterprising RAF commandant got together a pack of dog sentries for his station. Consisting of seven airedales and seven alsatians, they were all recruited from the Dogs' Home. They were given an allowance of 2d per day for meat—as much as was allowed for human beings—and otherwise subsisted on scraps from the mess. They were probably some of the best-fed dogs in the country at that time of acute food shortage.

Found, abandoned in a dustbin

Tommy Steele and his daughter reunited with their beloved pet, Tramp

Relations have always been good with the police!

Margaret, a stray that went to Abu Dhabi to become the cosseted pet of an oil sheik. She travelled by private jet

In September 1940, almost at the end of the first blitz, the Home received a direct hit. The bomb fell, incredible to relate when one remembers the extreme vulnerability of the Home's position between road and railways, the gas-works and power station nearby, exactly in the middle of the roadway that runs between the main gates—the only place, in fact, where it could do very little harm. Although it caused a good deal of damage, there was neither loss of life nor injury to man or beast.

In spite of the bombing that went on night after night, the general work of the Home continued as usual, but of course with a very depleted staff. A system of firewatching was set up among the staff so that there was a continuous rota, but Healey Tutt undoubtedly bore the brunt, as he always felt it was his particular responsibility and concern.

A flood of anxious pet-owners presented themselves at the Home, bringing with them their dogs to be destroyed, as the future looked so uncertain. Healey Tutt, however, with his invariable good sense and concern for the ultimate welfare of animals, pleaded with them to bide their time and see how things went. He explained to this seemingly never-ending queue of worried and distraught people that, once the dogs were dead, that was that; full of optimism, he added that nobody knew what lay round the corner. It is just as well nobody did, for those dogs were destined to live out their lives on short rations . . .

It was a terrible winter for everybody who remained in London. Night after night the wailing sirens sent up their unearthly rising and falling shriek to the skies, sending Londoners scurrying to their emergency beds in cellars and under staircases, and, in many cases, down to the deep tube stations, where iron bunk-beds ranged along every platform and a new sort of pattern of existence emerged for those who used them each night. Minutes after the sirens had been heard, the sky was filled with the uneven sound of the German bombers, followed by the terrifying scream and blast of the bombs themselves that brought death and terror right into the very heart of this country that had not suffered an actual military invasion for nearly a thousand years.

Dozens of incendiary bombs fell on the Dogs' Home but, as they rained through the skylights above the corridors that ran down the centre of the long kennels, they caused little damage, and were soon extinguished by the extremely efficient firefighting team that had soon developed from the group of men who took it in turns to stay up every night. The damage that was caused was temporarily repaired the next day in such a way as best could be devised with the shoddy and hard-to-obtain materials that were all that was available. This pattern of existence continued for weeks on end, until at last the first blitz ended. London showed under its repeated bombardment that civilian morale could be stiffened rather than broken by the savagery, and that an air bombardment required the back-up of an immediate land attack in its wake. This is where Hitler made his cardinal error in those early days.

Still the dogs poured in, and almost exactly the same numbers were recorded as those for the immediate pre-war years. Surprising to relate, the numbers of dogs that went to new homes were also about the same, in spite of all the difficulties during those years of privation.

Thanks principally to the good management of Lord Woolton, whom Winston Churchill appointed as Minister of Food, and to the courage and endurance of both our Royal Navy and the Merchant Navy, Britain did not starve. Woolton soon found, on taking office, that the people at the Ministry of Food knew nothing about publicity. They would produce a large poster that said: 'Let your shopping save our shipping.' What could that possibly mean to any ordinary housewife? So Woolton had posters printed and widely distributed that said simply and directly: 'Don't waste bread.' He found that to get the co-operation of the public it was better, instead of preaching at them, to tell them the facts, and people found wasting food were prosecuted. Arrangements were made for whatever was left over from the human table—and that was precious little—to be used for pigs and poultry:

Because of the pail, the scraps were saved,
Because of the scraps, the pigs were saved,
Because of the pigs, the rations were saved,
Because of the rations, the ships were saved,
Because of the ships, the island was saved,
Because of the island, the Empire was saved,
And all because of a housewife's pail.

However, people were still prepared to share their little with their pets, perhaps because those pets represented a sort of continuity and security that was sadly lacking in their lives, when death lurked round every corner and could rain from the skies at any moment. Most of the young men were away fighting, possibly never to return, and so the family dog and cat took on a new importance in the home.

On 16 April 1941 a land-mine fell on one of the gasometers that stands behind the exercising grounds. This could easily have spelt the end of the Dogs' Home—and, indeed, for half of Battersea. By one of those happy quirks of providence that seem to have lent a magic cloak of protection to the Home, very little damage was caused, apart from that of blast to the woodwork and to the windows, which in any case were boarded up for most of the war.

In 1941, sadly, a return had to be made to the old order that had prevailed all those years ago, before Queen Victoria had taken a personal interest in the Home and asked for an extension of a dog's stay from the then statutory three days. Food was ever more desperately short in the country, and it is amazing that Healey Tutt managed to feed the 145,000 dogs that passed through the Home during those five years. On examining the records closely, it becomes clear, however, that he took very little notice of this new three-day edict, three-quarters of the dogs being kept for nearly a week, just as they always had been during his time.

By 1943 the number of staff at the Home had been radically decreased as more and more men were called up, the age-groups rising each successive year as more and more younger men fell in the various fields of battle. Only the older staff remained, a pattern resembling that of the Great War, and only a limited number of new men—mostly ones who had been invalided out of the forces—were able to be recruited. In spite of all this, and in spite of soap rationing and the general shortage of everything needed to maintain standards, the Home was kept spotlessly clean, although maintenance was bound to suffer. Not only was it impossible to obtain paint in the quantities required by the Home, everything available was used immediately to do on-the-spot repairs of bomb damage.

The fire-fighting squad itself presented problems for poor Healey Tutt, for, ever-mindful of the welfare of his dogs, he hesitated to recruit people from outside; this would necessarily involve making a reciprocal arrangement with another band of fire-fighters, and he knew that anyone lacking experience in the handling of large numbers of dogs would be at a loss in an emergency. The authorities were totally unsympathetic—understandably feeling that they had far greater problems on their hands than stray dogs.

Fortunately Healey Tutt had always maintained extremely good relations with the police, and this was to stand the Home in very good stead for they proved a tower of strength. Not only did they give Healey Tutt wise advice, but, undoubtedly by a certain amount of adroit string-pulling behind the scenes, they helped over the maintenance of the absolutely essential petrol supplies. Poor Healey Tutt had been driven to go along and make an impassioned plea to a Captain Roberts at the Albert Bridge Flour Mills, sub-district manager of the Petrol Board, to ask to be allowed to maintain the same petrol ration as before, in view of the great distances that had to be covered by the vans daily—many diversions being necessary owing to bomb damage, as well as all the other difficulties—only to be told abruptly that the best way of dealing with the problem would be for each police station to have a mobile gas chamber where the dogs could be destroyed as soon as they were brought in. Eventually, mid-week collections were stopped; this, although saving petrol, led to a build-up of animals at the police stations, and longer journeys had in consequence to be made on subsequent days.

Healey Tutt scraped the barrel over his supplies of food, and he certainly did a good deal of what, for him and his dogs, was essential stockpiling, even though strictly speaking it was against the law.

Again through the kind offices of the Commissioner of Police, during the last year of the war the Dogs' Home drivers were listed under the Essential Works Orders, as it was found that older men simply could not manage the heavy work involved—this seems strange as nowadays the van work is done entirely by women. All the people employed at the Dogs' Home, like other workers all over the country, were called on to do extremely long hours and had to be available for fire-watching duties as well. The fact that in this country we had very few shirkers is a testimony to our grit and determination as a nation to survive.

A number of unclaimed stray dogs from the Home were taken by the War Dogs' school for training. It had been thought that tanks and aeroplanes and the wireless would finally banish the dog from battlefields, but it was proved without doubt that the dog served a greater purpose in the Second World War than ever before, being supreme in the fields of liaison, as Red Cross workers and as sentries.

German dogs sailed to earth by parachute and sought out and exploded landmines which had failed to be detected by conventional mine detectors, owing to the fact that in the later stages of the war the mines were housed in wooden or plastic cases. The dogs hurled themselves under tanks to destroy them with bombs strapped to their backs. It is difficult to imagine such an order being either given to or carried out by a British soldier who had trained his dog for warfare. British dogs carried poison gas canisters into enemy positions, succoured the wounded and carried messages across ground so heavily under fire that a man could not hope to get through.

In 1914, as we have learnt, the Germans had possessed more than 1,500 trained dogs, but in 1939 they entered the war with at least 50,000 highly trained animals. These dogs were subjected to rigorous German discipline, and eventually they 'passed out' to take their place in the German war machine—in other words, to place themselves totally at the disposal of their ruthless German commanders, who seem not to have had an ounce of pity or compassion in their make-up.

During the war, British dogs were trained to guard vital points against air-borne attacks, to track down parachutists and to undertake liaison work. They were trained to lay wires across country that was under concentrated fire, and to carry ammunition, as Red Cross workers, and as 'smellers out' of enemy position. An urgent appeal was made for dogs measuring from $1\frac{1}{2}$ to $2\frac{1}{2}$ ft at the shoulder and of a sombre colour, capable of carrying loads of at least half their own weight—hence the demand and the supply of a constant stream of alsatians and airedales from the Dogs' Home.

That Healey Tutt bore the brunt of the difficulties brought about in administering the Home during the war years is evidenced by the few records that still exist. He was an extremely conscientious man whose only concern was for the well-being of the dogs under his care, and also for that of his staff; but it is clear that, with only the War-Time Emergency Committee, he was left largely to struggle along by himself with very little backing from his Committee.

Ten days after the victory on the Western front, the time for the dogs to be kept was increased once more to seven days; and although this of course was good news up to a point, it provided almost insurmountable difficulties with regard to the provision of food and labour.

However, the war was virtually over, and at least the Dogs' Home had survived, almost unscathed.

11 Happier Days

Although the war was now over, and the Dogs' Home was no longer under the constant and only too real threat of immediate and complete annihilation, things did not return to normal for several years by any means. There still had to be a policy of make-do and mend for some time, as materials were virtually unobtainable, and priority was invariably (and understandably) given to human dwellings that had been war-damaged rather than to places intended for animals. Poor Healey Tutt struggled on, trying not only to make ends meet but to keep the fabric of the Home in one piece, the staff performing miracles of makeshift repairs. He was not only having these difficulties but was also suffering from the effects of the early stages of Parkinson's disease, which was eventually to force him into retirement.

The biggest problem that had to be faced in the immediate post-war years was still the acute shortage of food, which was being felt more and more. This was a vicious circle for, with the general domestic shortage, people were abandoning their pets in a most cruel and heartless way—few of them having the moral courage to take their animals to be put down painlessly, or even to make the effort to find them another home. They threw them out and the creatures eventually landed up in the Dogs' Home, where they provided correspondingly more mouths to feed . . . and there was less and less to feed them on. In spite of the fact that the war was over and shipping was now plying backwards and forwards across the oceans in comparative safety, Great Britain was destined to struggle for several more years with the food problem.

The numbers of dogs in the Home rose by 2,000 each year from 1945, until in 1948 there were 28,176 handled, with 53,000 visitors. Then, at last, there was a gradual decline so that there were only 12,000 by 1954.

There was also a sharp rise in the cost of foodstuffs, and the bills at the Home were found to have doubled since 1939. Fortunately donations were increasing, although subscriptions remained at a fairly low level, and legacies were beginning to accumulate, so that the investments looked quite healthy, and the income derived from them was substantial, going a long way towards paying the inevitably increased expenses.

The Duke of Portland, who had been President of the Home since Lord Onslow became Governor of New Zealand in 1889, died in April 1943, and the 10th Duke of Beaufort, whose father had been a Vice-President of the Home for many years until his death in 1924, was approached and asked to become President. The Duke of Beaufort, who has not only been Master of his own pack of foxhounds since his father's death, a family tradition that has been carried on for at least five generations, was also Master of the Horse, an appointment made by the Monarch, and one that he held from 1937 until 1978, longer than anyone else in history. Strangely enough, the Duke of Portland, the previous President, was also Master of the Horse from 1886–92 and then again from 1895–1905.

When the Duke of Beaufort became President of the Home it was the start of an association and interest that has lasted to this day. He paid his first visit to Battersea just before the end of the European war, and has gone down regularly ever since, often accompanied by the Duchess, who shares his great interest in and love for dogs. Several Battersea strays have gone down to Gloucestershire to grace—and to a large degree, to rule—the ducal home at Badminton.

Recently two Battersea dogs went one better. They were flown out to Geneva by private jet aeroplane to join the household of the Sudanese ruler of a territory larger than the whole of the British Isles. However, it is not every dog's good fortune to end up like that. To a dog that is lost or abandoned, any home at all is good enough. Unhappily, all too often their last glimpse of the world is from behind the bars of the kennels at Battersea.

In 1947, the entire office staff consisted of five people, and as the Home was open seven days a week this threw an even greater burden on the already overweighted shoulders of the

Secretary and his assistant, Mrs Witherow, who had been with the Home for twenty-five years.

In the kennel yard, Superintendent Ball and his assistant, Mr Carstairs, who had been at Bow until it closed during the war, still had to work with virtually a skeleton staff, in spite of the increase in the number of dogs they were handling.

By 1951, staff problems were intensified. There was a great call for unskilled labour in the factories that had sprung up all around the district, and that year also saw the opening of the Fun Fair in Battersea during the Festival of Britain year, that swept up the existing supply of casual labour on which the Home had grown to rely. 1951 also saw a country-wide epidemic of distemper and hard pad, and a thousand fewer dogs were sold during that year compared with the previous twelve months.

For many years it had been necessary to warn the public that, although there were many excellent animals for sale each day at the Home, the Committee could undertake no responsibility for them, nor give any kind of warranty. The importance of a personal visit to the Home when looking for a dog that had been lost was stressed, as identification of a particular one, however good the description or even photograph, was impossible for anyone except the owner.

In 1953, Mr Healey Tutt, whose wife had died two years before, was eventually obliged to retire on grounds of ill health, and he went out to South Africa to join his daughter. He lived there for several more years. He was a truly remarkable man, gentle, and, it would seem, easily put-upon.

Unfortunately his retirement was to bring some staff troubles, as Mrs Witherow had been led to believe by Sir Charles Hardinge that she would succeed Mr Healey Tutt as Secretary of the Home. The appointment of Lt. Commander Benjamin Knight in Healey Tutt's place led to the premature retirement of Mrs Witherow and to the resignation of Sir Charles. The new Chairman was Sir James Ritchie, Bart., who was also Joint Honorary Treasurer of the London School of Hygiene and Tropical Medicine, had various business interests in the fields of textiles and steel, and was President of his local branch of the British Legion.

Lt. Commander Benjamin Knight had spent most of his adult life at sea, first in the Merchant Navy and then in the

Royal Navy. He had broken his back in the Malta Convoy during 1942, eventually being invalided out of the Service in 1949.

He was to describe his introduction to the Home:

I'll never forget how I felt as, with my wife, I saw for the first time, the grey Home merging into the even Battersea surroundings. The smoke-belching Power Station deposited grit and filth everywhere, the trains seemed to roar from all directions over our heads, and the trunk road traffic rumbled all around us.

When he arrived, the kennels were very much as they had been built, but, owing to the war-time difficulties and the restrictions of materials that had existed ever since, there was rusty, peeling paint everywhere outside and, with fuel problems added to everything else, a cold dinginess inside. Commander Knight briskly set to work, putting in false ceilings and walls to keep out the damp and cold of the original stone, and the straw and sawdust beds were replaced by hardwood benches, similar to those used in Hunt kennels.

Commander Knight soon discovered that he could turn his hand to any job in the Home, and, after a staff dispute resulted in the walk-out of the entire force of drivers, he found himself driving one of the ten-ton clumsy green vans that lumbered around the streets of London in those days. Eventually he found that women were to prove better at that job than their male predecessors, as they cornered less violently, with less consequent sickness to their canine passengers. They also possess the happy knack of an instinctive knowledge of the right approach that should be used with their charges that can and do vary from coddled pekinese to savage guard dogs.

12 The Home and the Press

There has always been a stream of upsetting stories about the way in which dogs are abandoned, some being thrown out of cars onto motorways, some thrown into canals with bricks round their necks, and some even being put into dustbins. The keepers soon develop a sort of sixth sense when dealing with members of the general public, and can tell instinctively whether a good home is being offered or not. If not, then nothing on this earth will persuade them to let a dog go.

There have also always been some incredible coincidences concerned with the Home. For instance, one day a woman came in to report the loss of her chow chow, only to look out of the door and see the very dog walking by. One of the members of the Committee telephoned the Home as a last resort, as a friend had lost his sealyham and pekinese in Southampton. Those two dogs were at Battersea, and had even been put into the same cage as they seemed so fond of each other. I myself was asked to replace a much-loved Great Dane that had just died for a friend by a dog from the Home. It had to be a big dog, and preferably an Irish Wolfhound dog of about ten months old. The likelihood of such a dog being found in the Home on any particular day was so unlikely as to border on the absurd. Imagine my amazement when, on making enquiries of the Superintendent in the Yard, I was told that the only large dog available that day was—yes—an Irish Wolfhound dog puppy that appeared to be about ten months old.

To quote a collection of reports from the press cuttings books kept at the Home would be repetitive, and would often serve to make the work done there appear trivial, as much the same sad and happy stories appear over and over again. What is news today is already forgotten by tomorrow, and the same thing becomes news once more ten years later.

135

However, there are some stories, many of which have not reached the newspapers, concerning not only the dogs but also the people involved with every dog that appears in the Home.

Early in 1951 the two-millionth dog was handed in—two million. Two million dogs in under a hundred years. What a picture the number conjures up of the work that has gone on day after day in Battersea, by a band of truly dedicated people, dedicated not only to their charges but also to helping human beings. For behind every doggy tragedy often lies a human tragedy of greater or lesser degree—desperate little tragedies like that of the small dog seen curled up in the corner of its cage wearing a betasseled multicoloured knitted jacket. It had been brought in a day or two earlier by an old lady who could no longer afford to keep her companion, and therefore brought it to where she knew it would receive good care, and from where a home would be found that would guarantee that its days could be ended in comfort. She had knitted the little coat as a parting gift so that it would not catch cold in what she imagined to be the draughty kennels of the Home while it waited to be chosen.

A story appeared in the *Sunday Despatch* in the winter of 1952 when a stray alsatian bitch, which had been taken to the kennels lying at the back of a police station, broke free and started to bark and to rush around the charge room. First the station sergeant, then another sergeant, and finally three constables tried to capture her; but, terrified, she attacked and bit each of them in turn. They then gave up and called the Dogs' Home, when a single attendant arrived, captured the dog and took her away in a van. This little story depicts what might have been an ugly scene of fear and panic, when one recalls the Baker Street scandal of nearly a hundred years before, which provoked so much criticism of police methods in those days.

However, a nice story was carried by *The Star* a year or two later:

Mrs M Benson, an attendant at Battersea Dogs' Home, was called to Twickenham Police Station to-day to remove two stray dogs. When she arrived in a van, the dogs were there sure enough—a black terrier and an alsatian. The terrier hopped into the van quickly enough, but the alsatian refused to budge. Mrs Benson offered him some chocolate. The dog obligingly gobbled up a quarter of a pound, but still bared his teeth whenever she tried to move him.

After ten minutes Mrs Benson sought the help of a police-sergeant. 'I'm having an awful job with the alsatian,' she explained. Then her mistake was discovered, for one of the stray dogs had escaped, and the alsatian she was trying to take away was Storm the police dog.

A third story should be told here—that of Gus, the police alsatian that was delivered at the Dogs' Home as a stray by a police constable from his own station. The trouble began when a stray dog—a wolfhound called Wolfgang—was brought in and put in a kennel. At lunchtime, when the regular dog handler was off, a policeman was detailed to take the dog to Battersea. The stray and the police dog occupied adjacent kennels, and the simple fact is that the inexperienced young constable took the wrong dog. His Chief Inspector rather sheepishly explained that of course the police dog was not fully trained, or it would never have allowed itself to be taken.

A Mr Mattison made a business in the 1950s of training dogs for guard work on parcels and goods vans, at a time when compensation paid out by the Railway Executive for six months amounted to a staggering £2,200,000 for theft, loss or damage of goods. Police guards were mounted and hundreds of schemes introduced at marshalling yards and depots, and the use of highly trained guard dogs was particularly successful in the docks. British Road Services employed forty-two dogs on their strength in 1952, most of which had been recruited from Battersea. Mr Mattison's methods of training were quaint, but they evidently produced the required results. His assertion was that dogs had to hate their handler first, and then grow to like him. His methods were a direct contradiction to those used by the police, as they train their dogs entirely by kindness, as did Colonel Richardson back in the Great War.

One day a man came to the Home carrying in his arms a very young fox cub. He had been driving through Canvey Island in Essex when he saw a vixen strangled in a barbed wire fence, and there, whimpering beside her, was the little cub. Picking it up, he took it home, thinking he would soon find it a home. However, it was not as easy as he had thought, so finally he decided to try the Dogs' Home.

'Freddy' was an immediate success, becoming completely tame and quite famous during his stay, living on a diet of bread and milk and a quantity of fresh raw meat. Eventually Commander Knight had the bright idea of contacting No 12 Squadron, RAF, whose emblem is the mask of a fox. They were only too happy to adopt Freddy as their mascot, and, after a suitable presentation ceremony, off he went to Lincolnshire to join a live bat belonging to No 9 Squadron which had been presented to them by a Colonial Governor when their Squadron accompanied the Queen on an African tour. (No 12 Squadron got its emblem of the fox in 1926 when it was the first and only Squadron in the RAF to be equipped entirely with Fairey Fox machines.)

In 1954 a small brown mongrel with big brown eyes 'touched the heart of Britain', to quote the words used in the *Daily Mirror*. Smokey appeared on a television show, and the result was that dogs' homes all over the country were literally besieged by people wanting to offer homes to unwanted strays.

The Evening Standard ran a story headed: 'The Shaggy Dog Story that Saves Lives.'

Shaggy was such a hopeless sheepdog that his owner sold him. Now he and three other dogs, whose masters did not want him, are helping to cut down the number of road accidents by teaching children how to control their pets. They are members of the Canine Defence League road safety demonstration team. The other three are Flash, a mongrel who kept running away; Stevie, a poodle, who failed as a pet; and Laddie, a ten-year-old collie from the Battersea Dogs' Home.

Each year the dogs travel more than 15,000 miles by car giving demonstrations to schools and children's cinema clubs. Their trainer says: 'It's strange to think these dogs were of no use to anybody. As a team they're superb.'

Sometimes newspapers that are short of what is described as 'hard news' fall back on the undoubted sob-story value of the Dogs' Home.

It looked as though the fine Christmas presents young Stephen bought for his pet would stay unwrapped in a

138

bedroom cupboard. And Stephen, 13, was a sad boy as he gazed, chin in hand, from the high window of his parents' flat on Christmas Eve. The gifts were an embossed leather dog collar, a new lead, and a red ball which tinkled as it bounced. But the dog for whom they were intended was dead. What chance was there of a happy Christmas for Stephen now?

The day before, his black terrier, Chummy, had leapt after a pigeon on the window sill, and fallen fifty feet to the pavement below. The accident was reported to this paper, and someone remembered Chummy had won a consolation prize at our Flower and Country Show last summer. Wasn't there another story too? Didn't Stephen and his mother save Chummy's eyesight? Yes, they did. Obviously here was a boy who really loved animals and a home where they were welcome. That is why one of our reporters called on Stephen on Christmas eve, and why he had a happy Christmas after all.

Off went the reporter with Stephen in his car to Battersea. When it returned, the boy had his arms round a large fluffy brown mongrel. They had become friends on sight when they met in Battersea Dogs' Home. On Christmas Eve the dog slept in a warm basket in the kitchen, and next day he had his Christmas gifts along with the rest of the family and joined in the fun.

Many Battersea dogs have ended up as film stars, and most of them have become the property of either the star or someone on the set who has taken a fancy to them. One of these was Dolores, who acted in Graham Greene's *Across the Bridge*, which starred Rod Steiger and Noel Willman; in all the notices of the film it was said that the picture-stealing actress was a mongrel called Dolores. The most graphic description of Dolores' performance was contained in a report on the film carried by the *News Chronicle*:

The latest portrait in Rod Steiger's small but unforgettable rogues' gallery is the fugitive crook-financier of *Across the Bridge*. You may gauge the portrait's brilliance by the fact that its perpetrator just succeeds in stealing the picture from one of the most endearing bitches in screen-history—a mournfully unthoroughbred spaniel called Dolores, who was discovered in Battersea Dogs' Home and groomed specifically for co-stardom with Mr Steiger. St Sebastian never gazed skyward with so monumental a look of martyrdom as Dolores in her final anguish. Landseer never found a sitter whose nose was more moist with devotion. Had the film been a silent one she might have queened it over all comers; but though she can snarl and yelp and whimper as evocatively as any exponent of The Method, she cannot speak—and here Mr Steiger has the measure of her . . .

There is no doubt that people carry sentiment to great lengths, as is evinced by a newspaper story in 1957 reporting the arrival of a raven-haired Italian girl who had come to London to be 'nanny' to a mongrel of doubtful ancestry, formerly from the Dogs' Home. The owner of the dog introduced the Italian girl as Enoch's nanny, adding that the dog even slept in her bed. She went on to say that he wore a natty white cotton suit, tartan bow-tie and a dainty hankie in his pocket and had a party for some of his friends on his birthday, and a cake with blue icing and eleven candles. She added what was perhaps a superfluous statement: 'You know my husband thinks I am silly about dogs . . .'

A heart-touching story to offset the cloying sentimentality of the last is that of Peter and Paul. Peter was blind, and he was led everywhere by his devoted companion, Paul, both of them black labrador retrievers. They were brought into the Home together, and as they went down the corridors, Paul nosed Peter in and out of the doorways, carefully steering him around dustbins that lay in his path and, when in the pen, guided him to a bowl of water. This sad story had a happy ending though, for thanks once again to the *Daily Mirror*, the dogs were re-united with their owner.

For many years the Dogs' Home has looked after dogs for people serving prison sentences. One of these dogs found a wonderful home with the Duke and Duchess of Beaufort where, with the full consent of her convict owner, she ended her days in style, being the devoted companion of the Duke.

In the middle of stories of terror, famine and violence from all over the world, it is good to see headlines: 'Luxury of animal

'Sprechen Sie Deutsch?' 'Parlez-vous français?' 'Parliamo Italiano?' It was discovered that this dog understood only Welsh!

Bootsie was found on Charing Cross station guarding a pair of shoes from which he would not be parted. He now lives happily in a new home in Bristol and has abandoned the shoes

Dogs and cats are made
equally welcome at the
Home

How do you lose a dog of
this size?

welfare', 'For Lost Dogs, This is Like Utopia'. There are, however, schools of thought that feel that money devoted to the care of dogs should go instead to human beings; nevertheless, it is undoubtedly true to say that behind every tragic dog story there tends to be a perhaps even more tragic human story, and every dog story that ends happily carries its full share of happiness into the human world.

A story told in 1965 of a man who risked his life to rescue a dog from the tube line when death from the 630-volt live rail was only inches away is strongly reminiscent of one told in 1919 of two brave women. A dog had got itself into an almost inaccessible position on the Underground Railway, and was too terrified either to come out or to allow anyone to get near enough to rescue it. The two ladies arrived at Gloucester Road Tube Station and heard the dog howling; they were told that, although many attempts had been made to get it out and to feed it, all had been unsuccessful as the dog was mad with terror. As this was at the height of the post-war rabies scare there was some pardonable hesitation about approaching the animal.

However, when three days later the two women came to the station again, and still heard the demented howls of the little dog they decided that something must be done. So at one o'clock in the morning, when the current supplied to the rails had been switched off for the night, they arrived wearing overalls and carrying meat, a collar and a piece of rope. They quickly went into action, squeezing down a manhole, and then, with only the light of an electric torch, they crawled right along the whole length of the platform, coming all the way back again when the dog wriggled out of their grasp. At last they managed to catch him, and he was taken to Battersea. Had those two women performed such a feat nowadays, they would have found themselves facing a battery of cameramen from the television networks and reporters from the national press when they finally emerged from the manhole clutching the little dog.

A final story, ending in happiness, is that of a dog that became known as Bootsie. This dog was found on Charing Cross Station guarding a pair of shoes from which he refused to be parted. Eventually the policeman who was called in to deal with the situation found himself carrying both Bootsie and the shoes. The dog went to Battersea, still complete with shoes. Bootsie ended up with a family at Bristol, and the new owner made the 240-mile roundtrip to collect the dog, taking him back on her lap—still with the shoes. He now dominates their household, is weaned from the shoes, and provides a happy-ever-after story.

13 The Ultimate Rebuilding

When Commander Knight went to the Home, the numbers had dropped to 12,000 dogs a year, with periods of crisis at Christmas and at holiday times when there was always a great influx. The reason for this general fall in numbers was thought to be caused by the fact that people in London had given up their private houses after the war, and were now living in flats and council houses: in many of these pets were expressly forbidden.

At last, in 1955, the premises at Bow were sold for £7,500, more than this amount having been written off as a loss.

On 18 May 1956, much to the deep pleasure of all concerned with the Dogs' Home, Her Majesty Queen Elizabeth II graciously consented to bestow her Patronage upon the Home, continuing a tradition dating from the time when King Edward VIII, as Prince of Wales, first visited the Home in 1867.

The next ten years were to see greater changes than ever before in the aspect of the Home, for, just after the Centenary Celebrations in October, 1961, when the Duke of Beaufort unveiled a plaque commemorating the Centenary, a sub-committee headed by Commander Murray Cox, RN, was set up to report on the buildings as a whole. The first thing that was decided was that the offices and the Secretary's house should be rebuilt (in direct contrast to the report of that previous sub-committee set up for the same purpose in 1883, when the Secretary's house was last on the list). This was the start of a vast programme of rebuilding that stretched over twelve years, during which the whole of the premises have been rebuilt.

A publicity agent was employed to raise money for a Rebuilding Fund, circulars being sent to all police stations and to hundreds of schools, and programmes about the work carried out by the Dogs' Home appeared on television and sound

145

broadcasting programmes. A short film was made called *Little Dog Lost*, and this was shown at schools and clubs all around London (although recently this has been superseded by a much longer and totally professional version with a commentary by Johnny Morris that has been on circuit all over the country).

Stage one of the rebuilding scheme was finished by 1965, when the Commander and his wife were able to move into their new and modern flat over the offices from temporary quarters that had been rented for them locally; and, in 1969, stage two, the rebuilding of the actual kennels, was started. Various financial manoeuvres had to be made in order to provide the large sums of capital that were needed, and another appeal was launched by an auction sale of works of art arranged by Messrs Sotheby and Company.

The coming into use of these new kennels saw an immediate and dramatic change in the general health of the inmates, a change that has continued and improved as each successive stage of the building programme has been completed and another modern section of kennels has come into use.

In 1969 there was another change of Chairman, and Lord Cottesloe took the place of Sir James Ritchie. He was then also Chairman of the Committee responsible for the building of the National Theatre on the South Bank complex, so perhaps was better qualified than most for his job at the Dogs' Home. An oarsman and shot of international renown, his business interests were concerned with carpet manufacturing and warehousing, and he was Vice-Chairman of the Port of London for many years. He was also Chairman of the Tate Gallery and of the Arts Council of Great Britain, and of the Post-Graduate Medical Federation and of Hammersmith Hospital.

On becoming Chairman of the Dogs' Home, he arranged new contracts with the Metropolitan and City of London police that brought their payments up to date, and provided a basis for future negotiations, bringing those payments into line with the charges made for similar work by other organisations in different parts of the country.

In 1971 the final piece of land on the other side of the railway arches was bought from the British Railways Property Department—4,100 square feet at a cost of £1,400, and work was begun on the final stage of the rebuilding programme.

Altogether there are seven new kennel blocks at the Home,

which mark the end of a huge half-million-pound rebuilding programme, which leaves only the original railways arches—which cannot of course be touched, but have been modernised underneath—intact. The first phase comprised a new clinic, waiting-room, five kennel blocks, a whelping block and a cat house. These, the Beaufort Kennels, were opened by the Duchess of Beaufort in 1970 and cost £75,000.

In 1973, five more kennel blocks and a new staff mess-room were completed, costing £145,000. These, the Gloucester Kennels were opened by Princess Alice, Duchess of Gloucester, in October, 1975, inflation having rocketed the cost to £230,000.

The Dogs' Home now has 456 individual kennels and the multi-dog enclosures have been eradicated, although most of the new kennels can accommodate two healthy dogs when the need arises—and very often the dogs are happier with company and tend to pine less. Each compartment has thermostatic underfloor heating, and infrared health lamps have been installed. Hygienic, easily washable, fibreglass dog beds replace the wooden benches.

In one corner of the establishment, in high security isolation, are three kennels, with small exercise yards, that were designed and built for a specific eventuality. They are rabies pens built to Ministry of Agriculture specifications, ready for immediate use should this dread disease ever cross the English Channel from the continent, where it is on the increase.

In 1973, Commander Knight retired after twenty years during which time he did not spare himself in the service of the Home. In that time the Home has changed from the old-fashioned Victorian premises to the bright, modern, hygienic and superbly equipped buildings of today, where dogs have a real chance of being rehabilitated and found new homes. During the years that have followed the opening of the completed buildings there has been a dramatic change in the numbers of dogs destroyed in relation to the numbers that leave the Home. With the splendid facilities offered, every dog really has a chance of survival.

Colonel Henry Sweeney, MC—not surprisingly known to his friends as Todd—joined the Home in the autumn of 1973, and in the ensuing years is running it as it deserves to be run, with flair and ability, reflecting his brilliant career in the Green Jackets.

He has as his more than able lieutenant Mr Jack Winterflood, who came to the Home from the RAF in 1967, and his yard staff are led by Superintendent Bill Holmwood and Deputy Superintendent Fred Hearn.

An innovation in recent years has been the appointment of a Public Relations Officer, and in Mrs Olive Dawes it seems that once again the Home has the right person, seemingly tailor-made and destined for the work. Her dedication has always been outstanding, and she does not regard it as just another job to be done well, but shows real concern, not only for the animals, but for all the people with whom she deals. *

The Home is a truly friendly place and, although the heart is always touched by a visit, there is no longer the anguish. The dogs appear to have lost their agonised expressions and, instead, seem to be full of hope instead of despair.

---

* Tragically, Olive Dawes died the day those words were written; but perhaps the happy thing is that before she died she too, like Mrs Mary Tealby, was able to see the fruition of all her hard work.

Appendix 1: Your Battersea Dog

When you arrive home with your Battersea dog, you must not be disappointed if its immediate reaction to the new surroundings is not one of instant joy. It will take a little time for the animal to acclimatise itself, as dogs do not like changes at the best of times, and this particular dog will have had enough of these during the past week or two to last it a lifetime.

Put yourself in the dog's place for a minute. In the first place, you are lost—and nobody will ever know what agonies of mind you went through while you were wandering in the streets, seeking your master and your familiar surroundings, nevermore to find them. In all probability you had to sleep out, and rough at that, for a night or two, followed by a stay of up to twenty-four hours in a police station, where, although certainly you would have been kindly treated, the kennels do not exactly represent the canine Hiltons of the suberbs—more like a Blackpool boarding house: clean and no nonsense.

The following morning, a large red van would have arrived, and you would have been bundled fairly unceremoniously into it, attached by a chain to a hook, and then, after what could be quite a long journey picking up fellow sufferers from the various police stations on that day's list, at last you would have arrived at the Home. Once out of the van, there would come what you might find the indignity of a full veterinary-medical examination. Then according to those findings, you would have been allotted to a particular set of kennels, probably sharing a pen with a complete stranger. That in itself can be upsetting to a dog that has been used to being an 'only' (although in fact it is done on purpose, because dogs are naturally gregarious and tend to settle more quickly in company).

You would certainly find the food different: however good or bad your home standards, the food at the Home would be

149

bound to be different. A healthy dog will, by and large, always eat good nourishing food with verve and zest, provided it is presented in the form to which it accustomed. A dog in new surroundings is liable only to pick at what is offered on its plate, and does not get into the swing of mass feeding for several days.

That first night at the Home you would have been bound to wonder where you were and what was going to happen to you next; and when at last the dawn broke, to an accompaniment of a cacophony of discordant howls and barks, you would surely have spent a great deal of time either pressed against the bars of your cage, hoping against hope that the next person to come down the passage would be your own beloved master, or trying to get out. You might just have preferred to remain in your bed, feeling listless and very alone. Each time the footsteps came nearer, perhaps hesitated, a kind word, and then on again, your hopes would have been dashed.

Then would come the day when somebody arrived who showed some interest in you, you were taken out of your kennel and made much of. How you would have tried to please. How you would have licked their hand and wriggled with delight. Then, after another examination, out you would go, after all those searing experiences, into what, by now is the rather frightening big wide world.

So this is the dog you have brought back from the Home. You will have to give it time to settle down and acclimatise itself to yet another change of environment.

If the dog seems at all nervous, let new people come in quietly one by one, not all in a crowd, even if they do want to admire the new member of the family. The best of dogs could turn a little snappy after a week or two at Battersea, and it would be disastrous if the first thing it did was to give somebody a quick nip just because of a build-up of nervous tension.

As a new owner of a Battersea dog, you are going to need unlimited patience. With any normal new puppy patience is necessary, but with a Battersea dog it is essential. First you are going to have to gain the confidence of your new friend, engendering a feeling of complete security. That feeling will not come if there is constant chastisement. Bear in mind all the time the reactions of a normal dog. (My own two dogs behave as if they have been abandoned on an open windswept heath with only

Macbeth's witches for company when I have left them for half an hour or so—mind you, this is the same whether it is half an hour, two days or two weeks—and they have always had a completely settled life, with none of the terrible traumas of a Battersea dog.)

Your dog may be very quiet to start with—or perhaps over-lively. Do not worry, for the happy mean will come eventually, provided there is plenty of love and unobtrusive attention.

When you get home, try to resist the urge to plunge your new pet into a hot, soapy bath full of disinfectant. Dogs rarely enjoy a bath but most of them love swimming in a river or muddy ponds. That is quite one thing, and a nice clean bath is quite another. Content yourself with a good session with a brush and comb, but taking the greatest care not to pull a tangle or to upset the dog in any way. The keepers at the Dogs' Home will have already made a start on its toilet, if they have not found themselves too inundated with other duties, as is liable to happen at certain times of the year when there are more dogs coming in than usual.

Affection is what your dog will crave, and that is what you will wish to give with all your heart.

Make sure that there is plenty of fresh water available, and also opportunities to go outside. If the dog has already been house-trained, it will suffer agonies of mind if it cannot continue its clean habits. If it has not already been trained, then there is no time like the present . . .

Provide the dog with its own place, whether it be basket, old blanket or cardboard box. The important thing is that it should be draught-proof, and belong to the dog. It is usually wiser to start it off in a large cardboard carton that can be cut down to a convenient size and lined with a piece of old blanket or rug. It may well be that the puppy chewing habits have not yet been outgrown, and all these changes may cause a reversion to bad ways. It would be a great pity if a new basket was ruined just because the dog felt lonely or insecure during the first night.

Try to resist the impulse to make your own bedroom available—unless it is your firm intention to continue the habit—for you will regret it in the end.

Let it be repeated that the dog may or may not be house-trained—but you will soon find out! If not, then a routine

151

started at once and followed closely will help it to become an acceptable member of the household from the start. Outside after every feed, and then at regular intervals during the day, but more especially first thing in the morning and as late as possible at night. Never take the dog out of your own garden during the first weeks without using a lead. Always bear in mind that a labrador-type dog can clear a six foot wall, and a small terrier can scratch and burrow its way to freedom if left unguarded.

Be sparing with food at first. A little minced meat, either cooked or raw, mixed with some fine puppy meal and perhaps a beaten egg will probably be acceptable. Offer it dry at first, and then moisten it with a little gravy if the dog seems reluctant to eat it. You will probably find that two small meals a day will be the best at first. Then when the dog has settled down, these can be contracted into one larger meal at a time that suits your household—but preferably in the early evening. Dogs digest their food better if they are allowed a long sleep after eating. You may need to hand feed it for the first few days, but do not worry. This habit is easy to break once you have gained its confidence. Some dogs like to have a little something when you are having your own breakfast, such as a saucer of milk, a beaten egg or some cereal. Feeding from the table or between meals is a bad habit, and should never be started.

If the dog is thin, then the daily meal will need to be supplemented, but if, on the contrary, it shows a tendency to put on weight quickly, then stick to the once-a-day rule. Of course, if you have taken a puppy, then it should have three or four meals a day until it is at least three months old, and then two meals a day for the next six months.

Limit human friends at first, and keep other dogs away altogether. A clean bill of health from the Dogs' Home—and you would not have been allowed to take the dog away if they had found anything wrong that was immediately discernible—does not mean that a disease is not being harboured that takes longer than the seven days that the dog must, by law, have been in the Home to incubate and make itself shown. It would be impossible for the Veterinary Surgeon or the keepers at the Home to detect such an illness before the symptoms manifested themselves. A dog that is kept with a family is under constant surveillance, and the owners would notice immediately any change in the normal pattern of behaviour and habits. But the staff at the

Dogs' Home have no standard of measurement. They cannot possibly tell whether a dog is naturally quiet, liking to sleep most of the time, whereas in a dog known to be lively, those symptoms would immediately give rise to suspicions that all was not well.

If you do not already know of a good local veterinary surgeon, ask your most sensible dog-owning friends—not the ones who rush off to the vet if their little treasures give a single cough or sneeze—and they will probably be able to give you advice.

Telephone the surgery and explain that you have a dog from Battersea and would like a home visit. This is a warrantable expense, and is a sensible precaution from both yours and the vet's point of view. Should your dog unhappily be harbouring something, you will thus ensure not only that it is caught in the early stages, but also that it is not passed on to the other dogs waiting in a crowded surgery.

If the dog proves to be perfectly well, then ask the vet to worm it and give him what he recommends in the way of immunisation jabs. Do not let the dog mix with others in between injections, as that is the most vulnerable time to infection.

One of the first things you must do is to choose a name for your dog. Consider very carefully what this is to be, bearing in mind that fact that he must learn it as quickly as possible. His original name may have been anything from Sebastian to Spot, and, although dogs are quick to learn a new name as a rule, it is kind to make it as easy as you can. Bear in mind, too, that in all probability you are going to have to bellow the name at the top of your voice in the company of other dog-owners. 'Dinky' reverberating round the local park may make people stare a little, and will certainly embarrass your children. Do not forget, either, that a ten-week old woolly bundle may grow into a leviathan—the size of the paws at that age is a fairly good indication of the eventual size of the fully-grown dog. It would be a pity if a potential St Bernard were called Small or Tiny. Equally, a middling-labrador-sized dog is going to sound silly called Goliath.

When you take the dog for its first walk, try to make it a time of real enjoyment. Be very wary indeed of letting it off the lead until you are absolutely certain that not only does it know its name but that you have already forged a bond of friendship, so that it is likely to come to you when called.

It would be a good idea to enlist the help of a friend who has

153

an obedient dog, one that always comes immediately when called, for a good example at this stage is invaluable. When your own dog sees the other returning obediently to its master, then it is likely to do the same thing. Choose your friend with a dog very carefully, for nothing would be more disastrous at this stage than to see the two dogs disappearing happily into the distance.

Some simple obedience training in the garden or elsewhere on the end of a long piece of clothes line pays off. Call the dog from a short distance, and when it comes, even if wriggling reluctantly on its stomach, as long as it is actually coming towards you, this is the time for a reward. Titbits can be a menace, but they have their place in the order of things, and this is one of them. This does not come under the heading of bribery—it is called 'reasonable encouragement'.

Above all, enjoy your dog, for you will find that you have a friend for life—the dog's life, that is. Battersea dogs have a particularly marked tendency to devotion, and this is one time in life when you will have been able to buy love.

Appendix 2:
Whittington Lodge and its Cats

Mark Twain, the celebrated nineteenth-century American writer, said once that if man could be crossed with the cat, it would improve man but deteriorate the cat.

Cats as well as dogs play a part in the Battersea scene, one of the principal features of the yard being a charming building seen immediately on arrival and maintained in its original shape as it was designed by Clough Williams-Ellis the Edwardian architect in 1906. This little building, which now houses the staff quarters, is called Whittington Lodge, but for many years it was used as a shelter for stray cats. The Home took cats under its wing as long ago as 1882, and a few cats were accepted as boarders right back in the Holloway days, although that was found to be unpracticable, as conditions were far from easy in the cramped space at the Home's disposal.

Nowadays the cats are housed in a lovely modern building set behind the dog kennels, so that the nervous ones are not made over-aware of their canine companions in distress. Here, by an ingenious stacking arrangement, each cat has its own draught-proof compartment, which has a little door at the back opening on to a common large compound that affords them, if not a feeling of complete freedom, at least a chance to stretch their legs and climb and jump about on the branches provided—rather like the monkey house in a zoo.

The stay of cats in the Home is not limited by statute, as cats do not have legal rights as such, only being classified—together with camels!—as domestic animals, and by law treated as any other form of movable property. This means that the owner has the protection provided by the law in respect of absolute ownership, and they remain his property even when lost and straying. It is also covered by the law governing animals by the Protection of Animals (Anaesthetics) Act, 1954, whereby it is illegal to perform any operation on a cat without an anaesthetic, with the exception of castration for a kitten under six months old. The Performing Animals (Regulation) Act, 1925, also applies to the cat, whereby no person may train any performing animal nor exhibit any such animal at any entertainment to which the public is admitted, whether on payment or not, unless he is registered with the county or borough council of the place where he resides, and is subject to the rules that apply. Any constable or other person authorised by the local authority may enter and inspect any premises where performing animals are trained, exhibited or kept, at all reasonable times. The chances of this law being related to cats is rather remote, in view of the fact that cats appear to be one of the few animals that are completely untrainable. They do what they want when they want and how they want—and if that happens to be what their owner wants, then he is fortunate indeed.

The boarding of cats as a business in any premises, including a private dwelling, requires a licence issued by a local authority, and here again the premises are liable to be inspected at any reasonable time by a local authority officer or a veterinary surgeon.

Cats are also protected by section 1 (3) of the Larceny Act, 1916, when it became an offence to steal them, their value being decided by their owner.

The most important relationship that the cat has to law is in regard to its importation into the country, where it is bound by the same quarantine regulations that apply to a dog, and must undergo six months' quarantine at a registered premise. These regulations are, of course, rigidly controlled, and the only exceptions, which have to be specifically declared on an importation licence, are for (1) imported dogs or cats intended to be re-exported within forty-eight hours of landing; (2) *bona fide* performing cats or dogs. It is by now generally known through a propaganda campaign mounted by the Ministry of Agriculture that the unlawful landing of a dog or cat renders the offender liable not only to prosecution under the Diseases of Animals Act, but also to the penalties imposed on persons importing prohibited goods under the Customs Acts, and under these Acts the animal itself may be forfeited. This means that it can be ordered to be immediately destroyed, and only rarely is it allowed to be returned whence it came.

The relationship of man with cat is as interesting and as important in our study of the providing of succour and shelter for them, as is the relationship of man with dog. The cat has been revered from time immemorial, playing a part in man's religious life as well as in his superstitious fears, before it became his friend and companion to the degree that it does nowadays. It was first domesticated in ancient Egypt, and was used to keep rats from the grain; but such was its personality that it was not long before it was being worshipped as a deity.

It is fascinating to learn that both the ancient Egyptians and the Chinese, who were the next to domesticate the cat, called it by an onomatopoeic name. In Egypt it was *miu*, and in China it was and still is *mao*. In fact, all over Europe the word for the cat has a similar sound, deriving from the original Greek *katta*, now *kata*.

Their most likely ancestor is the African wild cat, which is about three feet long from the nose to the tip of its tail and is thus larger than the average domestic cat. It has long legs, a lean and sinuous body, and a long, thin tail; the back of its ears are a vivid rust colour, and its coat varies from reddish or sandy buff to greyish brown, according to its habitat. It has beautiful dark-rimmed eyes, which is perhaps why the ancient Egyptian beauties lined their eyes.

There is another theory, which is strongly supported, that the common domestic cat descends from the European wild cat, which is a different shape from the African one altogether. Greyish-brown with a barred tail and striped body, it is much the same size as the African wild cat, but has a wider face, longer fur, and a bushier tail. It is impossible to tame, even if raised from kittenhood in an entirely human environment. It is, of course, possible that both theories are correct, and that the European cat came from the European wild cat, and the more exotic Oriental and middle-eastern ones derived from the African wild cat.

The Egyptians had long venerated the lion, and it is likely that it was the lion-like qualities, with its positive genetic relationship, and the aloofness of the cat that first

157

attracted them to it as an object of worship. Who has experienced the inscrutability of the yellow or green unblinking gaze of a cat without the feeling that some mystery lies behind? Positive evidence of the cat's domestication is abundantly available from 1600BC onwards. Tomb paintings show cats sitting beneath their owner's chairs, and they are portrayed eating fish, gnawing bones, and playing with one another.

Cats also have a part in Greek mythology. There is a story of the flight of the Greek gods to Egypt to escape the monster, Typhon. Zeus, the chief god, fled in the guise of a ram; Apollo, the sungod, went as a crow; Hermes, the messenger, as an ibis, a bird rather like a spoonbill; Aphrodite, the goddess of love went in the unlikely guise of a fish; while Aries, the god of war, was perhaps more suitably changed into the form of a boar. It was Artemis, the moon goddess, patron of hunting, who made her flight disguised as a cat.

This Greek myth was much later than the cult of the cat in Egypt, but, as it was related by Greek historians as an ancient religious legend, it is possible that the two early cultures had been intertwined with the history of their gods.

The cat was the central figure in the cult of Bast at Bubastic, the ruined remains of which town can still be seen in the lower valley of the Nile. Bast was a cat-headed female goddess, and she was to lead much later on to the identification of women—and particularly of witches, something mysterious—with cats. Bast gradually took on the head of a cat, because originally she was the lion-headed goddess of fertility, motherhood, happiness and comfort. Cats appear on amulets which young married women hung on the walls of their house and to which they prayed for the same number of children as the cat had kittens.

Cats are noted for their beauty and the grace of their movements, and for their love of warmth and luxury. These are all characteristics that are associated in the mind with attractive women.

In ancient Egypt, the cat enjoyed divine protection, for to kill one was to court the death penalty. Its image was reproduced over and over again and then worn to ward off evil spirits. When a cat died, the Egyptian family was expected to go into mourning, shaving off their eyebrows, and mummifying it,

A happy ending awaited this racing greyhound, abandoned with a note on his collar requesting that a good home be found for him

An unsolicited gift sent to Edward Heath, then Prime Minister

later entombing it with a carved replica of its head. It was often encased in a bronze or gold casket in exactly the same way as the ancient Pharoahs, together with food and playthings for its sustenance and pleasure in its afterlife. For cats that lived in temples dedicated to the god, Bast, there was a public funeral when people lamented and wept aloud and beat their breasts for days.

At the end of the last century, more than a quarter of a million cat mummies were uncovered at Beni Hassan, providing very firm evidence of the place that the cat took in the life of the ancient Egyptians. These corpses were destined to have a very mundane end, for a merchant in Alexandria shipped most of them to Liverpool, and the cargo was sold locally to farmers as fertiliser. This is counted as one of the tragedies of archaeology, for only one skull remains in the British Museum out of a consignment that amounted to nineteen tons.

The ancient Greeks did not subscribe to the cult of cat worship, but Plutarch, the historian, mentioned them when writing of Egypt, saying that the Egyptians believed that a male cat represented the sun and that a female cat was symbolic of a goddess of the moon—hence the connection with the Greek goddess, Artemis. He also commented on the belief that cats are both good and evil, a belief that is held to this day in the minds of many people.

It is possible that the belief that the cat has nine lives may spring from ancient pagan Greek myths. To a superstitious and comparatively unsophisticated people, the ability of a cat to survive dangerous falls and many near-fatal accidents, due to its extraordinarily developed physical co-ordination and muscular control, must have seemed like magic. The Greeks, after all, believed that the sun and the moon created animals, the sun creating the lion and the moon the cat. They also thought that the little, swift-moving grey evening clouds were mice being chased off by the quick paws of the glowing cat— the moon—as it rose and night fell.

It was Greek traders who were responsible for the spread of the cat population across the world for they made a lucrative business of smuggling the precious animals into other countries. They worked with Phoenician traders and some unscrupulous and extremely courageous Egyptians, for the penalty if they were discovered was death; and between them they established the cat in middle eastern and Asian countries.

Much later, the Etruscans, the ancient inhabitants of Tuscany in Italy, had pet cats, as did the Romans. Although Julius Caesar was a notorious cat-hater, it was his troops who brought the cat into the rest of Europe, and particularly into these islands, although there is a theory that they appeared in Cornwall at an earlier date, brought in by Phoenician tin traders.

It was the accidental killing of a cat by a Roman soldier in Alexandria that started an Egyptian rebellion against Rome. The Romans never worshipped the cat, but they greatly respected it for its hunting abilities, and used its image as a design on their flags and banners. When they went to Holland, they called a fort *Cat Vicense*, known down to this day as the cat's town or *Kattewyk*. It was perhaps the independent spirit of the cat that led the Romans to use it as a symbol of liberty, for Roman legions setting out to defend their freedom had outline cats blazoned on their shields and banners.

Just before the Christian era, some Egyptian rites were introduced into pagan Rome, and the Egyptian goddess, Isis, was worshipped. Paintings were found of the Roman rites in a small town near Naples, and these included a rattle-like musical instrument called a sistrum that was shaken to ward off evil spirits, on the top of which was carved the head of a cat.

Later there were Italian Christian legends about the infant Jesus and a kitten, and it was said that a cat gave birth to kittens underneath the manger at the same moment at which Christ was born.

Going east, one of the ancient beliefs held in Burma and Siam was that the soul of a person who attained a high degree of spirituality in this life on their death entered the body of a cat. This provided a simple form of temporary purgatory, and was the means by which the soul passed into paradise.

Three hundred years ago a Burmese order of monks had sacred cats that played a prominent part in their ceremonies. Siamese cats have also taken part in religious rituals, and in many temples, silken black animals with enormous golden eyes are often still kept in gilded cages, where they lie on gorgeous cushions, deigning now and then to receive the offerings brought to them by the faithful. A Siamese legend says that a god once picked up a cat by the scruff of its neck, and hence the

Siamese cat has a typical shadowy patch on the back of its neck, which, it is supposed, denotes the hand of the god. A live cat was buried with the body of any deceased member of the royal family; but it is comforting to learn that the tomb was pierced with small holes so that the animals eventually were able to worm their way free. As soon as the cat emerged, the temple priests believed that the soul of the royal personage had entered the cat's body, so the fortunate animal was destined to be treated with that reverence reserved for princes for the rest of its natural life. Even as lately as 1926, at the coronation of the new king, the cat supposedly carrying the soul of the previous king, was carried ceremoniously by members of the court in the procession.

The Chinese Buddhists believe that the cat stands as a symbol of self-possession, a trait much to be desired. They also believe that a cat with a light-coloured coat will bring silver to its owner, and one with a dark-coloured coat will bring gold. There is an ancient legend that says that when the Buddha died a cat caught and ate a rat which was on its way to get medicine that would have effected a miraculous cure; hence the cat was barred from the funeral.

Chinese farmers, according to the Chinese *Book of Rites*, worshipped a cat called Li Shou. When the crops were safely harvested, the farmers held festivals and made sacrifices to this cat-god in gratitude for killing and eating mice and rats that might have destroyed the crops.

The ancient Chinese feared a beast known as a cat spectre. It was believed that women often served these demons, and this may have led credence to the belief that witches and cats are habitually associated. It was thought by the Chinese that cats in the form of these spectres killed human beings, whose possessions were then magically taken to the dwelling place of the demon cat. It was also believed that people changed into cat spectres after death and then tried to revenge themselves on their enemies.

The common name for a cat in Japan means 'jewel', and they have a good-luck charm in the form of a sitting cat with a paw raised to its ear. This little figure has a charming story connected with it. There was once a very poor temple of Gotoku-ji where the monks were poverty-stricken. One day, some noble Samurai warriors were riding by on their caparisoned horses, when they saw a cat, which was also lean and hungry, with its paw raised to its ear, seemingly beckoning to them. They stopped and followed it into the temple and, as they entered, heavy rain fell, so they stayed to shelter, and the chief priest gave them tea and talked to them about his faith. Later on, one of them returned to the temple, was instructed in the faith, and eventually endowed it and rebuilt it magnificently. There is even now a small shrine to this cat in the grounds of that temple of Cotoku-ji, just outside Tokyo, where visitors go to pray that they may have good fortune and prosperity.

Cats followed the Crusaders back from the Holy Wars, no doubt having proved their ability to keep the camps free of rats and mice, but the actual adoration of the cat waned with the spread of Christianity. Eventually it was to become a creature that was feared and tormented because of its supposed connection with witches and the devil, until in the fifteenth century it came near to extinction. Witch hunts abounded, motivated by mass hysteria, and for hundreds of years human beings were to be tortured and put to death, together with their innocent pet cats.

However, in the eighteenth century, mercifully this persecution declined, and gradually the cat rose in estimation again until eventually it became a favoured pet once more. It is interesting to recognise the fact that a black cat is still thought to be a symbol of good luck, and there are hundreds of superstitions all over the world concerning good or bad luck that is thought to be brought either by black or by white cats.

I do not subscribe to the school of thought that thinks a cat is an aloof, independent animal, mindful only of its own comfort and unconcerned with its human owners. Aloof and independent, yes, but most of the cats I have had and have known, although being comfort-loving to a degree, have been closely attached to their families, in very much the same way as a dog. Unlike the dog, the amount of affection a cat gives to its owners tends to be dependent on the affection and attention it receives from them. Therefore, when you take your Battersea cat home, you are taking what is going to be potentially a faithful, if not obedient, friend. It will grace your hearth and give you love, companionship, and comfort when you need it, probably for a great number of years, for cats are long-lived animals, as long as they

164

do not stray or get themselves killed by the alarmingly increasing amount of traffic we endure.

If you live on a main road or in a large block of flats, think very carefully indeed before you commit yourself to having a cat. You may find that a budgerigar or a canary is more suitable, or even a hamster, guinea pig or pet rabbit, all of which can be extraordinarily good company if brought up in a friendly, loving way.

If your cat does show a propensity to stray, give him a collar with an inset of elastic bearing your name and address. The elastic may save his life if he gets hooked in a tree, and on the collar he can carry a little bell, if it does not drive you mad, which will serve as a warning for birds. (If taken in hand early enough, it is possible to teach a kitten by suitable chastisement to ignore birds. But you have to be very careful indeed when punishing a cat, as it is only too easy to terrify it, thus turning it away from you forever.)

By all means provide your cat with a bed, but it will not necessarily use it. The majority of cats at Battersea tend to ignore their nice beds, and lie cosily instead on the sawdust that is intended for quite another purpose. Most cats will seek out any warm place, preferably plump in the centre of somebody else's bed, placing themselves in such a position as to ensure the maximum amount of comfort for themselves and discomfort for the human occupant. Beds should therefore be taboo. My own cats, however, are quite capable of beating on the bedroom door incessantly and imperiously until I am sometimes driven to open it, and resign myself to the rest of the night spent on the edge of the bed, or curled like a figure S.

Cats love typing. The movement of the carriage slowly across, and then rapidly back, is fascinating to them, and my black cat is at this moment sitting on the table and trying to move the space bar with her nose.

Cats also like to get themselves shut in cupboards or locked rooms, and then they cause a crisis in the household by their non-appearance at mealtimes. They rarely wail when they are shut in cupboards, for they are far too comfortable, but they are past masters at slipping past and miaowing pitifully on the wrong side of the door you have just slammed shut and locked, when you would have been prepared to swear they were somewhere quite different. It is true that they are very sure-footed, but please do not let them sit on high outside windowsills, as cats have been known to fall, and they do not, as is often thought, always land on their feet—and even if they did, from a height they would get a terrible jarring.

Cats should, as a rule, be fed once a day, and food should not be left about for them to eat at will. If you wish them to hunt, that is the one thing that will stop them; and, in any case, you will generally find that the food has been eaten by the dog with disastrous digestive consequences.

As with the dog, fresh water should always be available, and they love their daily saucer of milk. There are dried cat foods on the market which are designed to be eaten with a liberal drink of water. The instructions are clearly written on the packets but, alas, cats cannot read, and no cat will drink water because you think it ought to. It will only drink water, or do anything else for that matter, because it wants to.

They are very sensitive animals, and if they are suffering from persistent sickness and/or diarrhoea, or if their coat starts dropping out, do not rule out the possibility of nervous debility caused by some upset. Your veterinary surgeon will be able to prescribe a mild tranquiliser that will put matters right.

Cats seem to be clever at selecting their own diets, but they thrive on tinned cat food, so do not allow them to dictate that they will eat only the best fish. My black cat used to be adept at persuading a collection of old ladies that she was half-starved, sitting on our garden wall holding her sides in. These dear old ladies walked miles to bring little packets of delicious fish that my children would have enjoyed. The moment the feast was over and the little old ladies had disappeared around the corner, the cat puffed herself out to her normal proportions, and then went off to con someone into giving her a dish of cream. We have recently moved, and she is already starting the old routine. Cats are clever and are not to be underestimated.

Long-haired cats need grooming, which is a tedious process, but necessary if it is not to swallow large balls of indigestible fur, which it will then throw up on your best carpet at the feet of your cat-hating friends.

Should you suspect that your cat has fleas, use only flea powder specially designed for feline use. DDT is poisonous, and cats lick themselves constantly, so if you have dusted them with DDT they are in danger. Never be tempted to use a vacuum cleaner on a cat: you will terrify the animal and damage its skin.

Cats do, alas, scratch furniture, and the only way to stop them is by shouting at them whenever you see or hear them doing it. Prevent them from ever going into rooms where you do not want the upholstery damaged; allow them in only when you yourself are going to be there. That sounds negative advice, but it is the only way. Remember, cats only do things that they positively want to do.

Before we talk of illness, it is necessary to consider the appearance and behaviour of a cat in good health. As long as the cat is eager and hungry at its appointed—and, if possible, regular—mealtimes, then there is not much wrong with it. If it becomes listless, you must watch it for other symptoms, such as runny eyes or nose. If a cat eats voraciously, but still seems hungry and loses weight, you must suspect worms, and get a suitable worming tablet from your vet.

The normal temperature for a cat is 101–2 °F (38.3–38.9 °C) and its pulse, which is most easily felt in its thigh, should be eighty strong and even throbs to the minute. Do not worry unduly if the pulse is higher than this, as it may race owing to being handled in this way. It is when it is very slow that you have cause for concern, and you should watch the cat carefully, taking it to the vet if the symptom persists.

Have your cat immunised against feline enteritis, one of the most infectious diseases of the cat world, and from which a simple shot can give permanent immunity.

Do not be afraid to take your cat away with you. If they are provided with a cat basket or box designed for the purpose, out of which they can see but cannot escape, they will travel very well, although sometimes an occasional cat will be prone to travel sickness. Do not feed such a cat for at least four hours before the journey, make sure it is lying on plenty of newspaper (and that you have more spare in the car) and all should be well. If you have to take the cat out of its basket for any purpose on a journey, make absolutely sure that all the car doors and windows are tight shut while you do so. Nothing is more slippery than a frightened cat.

The most important advice of all is to enjoy your cat, enjoy its grace and beauty, and be grateful for its love, warmth and companionship.

Acknowledgements

Material from the Royal Archives is published by gracious permission of Her Majesty the Queen. References:

1 RA PP 1/6/9
2 RA PP 1/6/31
3 RA PP 1/6/37
4 RA PP 1/6/36
5 RA PP 1/6/45
6 RA PP 1/6/2
7 RA PP 1/6/4
8 RA PP 1/6/7
9 RA PP 1/6/39
10 RA PP 1/6/40
11 RA PP 1/6/41
12 RA PP 1/6/42
13 RA PP 1/6/33
14 RA PP 1/6/40, 1/6/41

Index